New Nations and Peoples

Syria Lebanon Jordan

Syria Lebanon Jordan

JOHN BAGOT GLUBB

with 69 illustrations and 10 maps

WALKER AND COMPANY
NEW YORK

© Thames and Hudson 1967

All rights reserved. No portion of this work may be reproduced without permission except for brief passages for the purpose of review

Library of Congress Catalog Card Number: 67-21589

First published in the United States of America in 1967 by Walker and Company, a division of Publications Development Corporation

Printed in Great Britain by Jarrold and Sons Ltd., Norwich

Contents

List of Maps

Introduction

Except in the most literal sense, Syria, Lebanon and Jordan cannot be said to be new and emergent nations. It is true that independent nations, in the modern sense, have not previously existed bearing these names and occupying precisely these territories, but under whatever political institutions, highly civilized people have lived in these areas for thousands of years.

Unfortunately, however, to most British and American readers the expression new nations conveys an impression of uncivilized people to whom it is our duty to impart the blessings of our culture. In the case of Syria, Lebanon and Jordan such an idea is most emphatically not applicable. Human history can be traced, with more or less accuracy, for some five thousand years. Of these, Syria was in advance of western Europe in civilization and culture for four thousand five hundred years. Only during the last five hundred years has the West taken the lead. If, therefore, we think of our history in thousands of years, it is we, rather than they, who are new and emergent.

It is true that, in the last century and a half, the West has forged ahead of the world in mechanical and manufacturing skills which have produced wealth of which men had never before even dreamed. But we are in error if, in our pride at our material achievements, we speak as if no other race had ever before been wise, cultured or civilized.

Another difficulty arises when we refer, even if briefly, to the history of these ancient lands. If we wished to be purists, we could say that Syria, Lebanon and Jordan only came into existence after the Second World War and thus have only some twenty-one years of history. But if we did in fact adopt this approach, we should be

7

utterly unable to understand anything of the situation today. For the institutions, the traditions, the religion and the whole mentality of these ancient peoples are the product of five thousand years of history.

Yet, incredible as it may seem when we consider it seriously, most of us seem to make just that mistake. We appear to assume literally that these are new nations, like new-born babies, whose characters can be moulded by us their parents. Or, to vary the metaphor, that we are dealing with a *tabula rasa* – a clean slate – on which it is our duty to inscribe our ideas, our traditions and our systems of govern-ment. I have preferred to submit to the reader a brief summary of the past history of these peoples, as being the only method of forming any idea whatever of the situation today.

To attempt thus to skim over long periods of history presents us, however, with another, even though it be a minor, difficulty. Not only do the names change, but at different periods one name may be applied to different areas. The name Syria is a case in point. It has sometimes been used for the whole area now included in modern Syria, Lebanon and Jordan. At other times it has been used for Syria and Lebanon or again for Syria and Trans-Jordan. In general, when dealing with the whole area between the Peninsula of Sinai and Asia Minor, I have used the geographical expression Syro-Palestine. This includes Syria, Lebanon, Palestine and Trans-Jordan.

As I have already stated, I believe it to be quite impossible to understand the situation in these lands without at least a superficial glance through their history. In fact, we find the same racial and geographical factors repeating themselves again and again for five thousand years and even today exerting exactly the same pressures as they did at the dawn of history.

Unfortunately, as history has been taught in the West for five hundred years, we are told at school a little of the history of Greece and Rome and from there we jump to the history of modern Europe. The many intervening centuries during which Muslim nations led the world are never included in our curriculum. Our utter ignorance of the past history of these peoples has been largely responsible for our many mistakes in our relations with them.

8

If anything in this little book can enlighten the reader or, better still, whet his appetite to study Arab history more deeply, the time which I have used to write it will have been well spent indeed.

I wish to acknowledge the assistance which I have received from my friends, most particularly from Albert Hourani, Fellow of St Antony's College, Oxford, from Professor P. J. Vatikiotis, of the Centre for Middle Eastern Studies, London University and from Sir John Richmond, of the Centre for Middle Eastern Studies, University of Durham.

J. B. G.

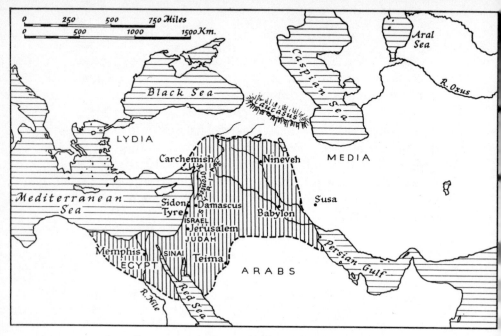

The Assyrian Empire of Nineveh 859–612 BC

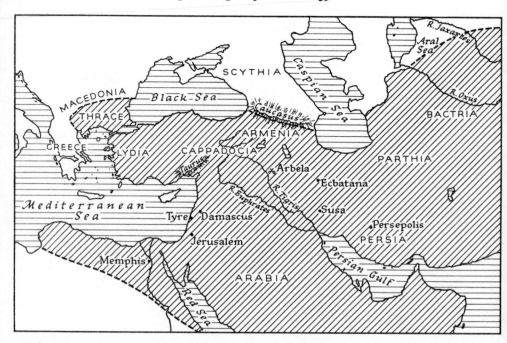

The Persian Empire 535–330 BC. (Note: The empire extended east to the River Indus)

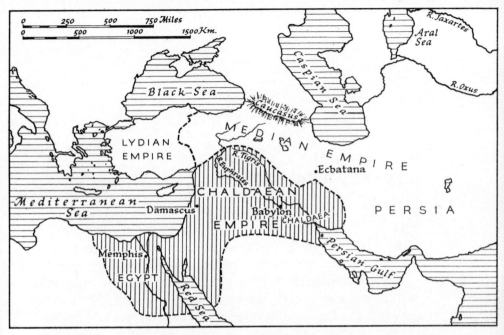

The Chaldean Empire of Babylon 612–538 BC

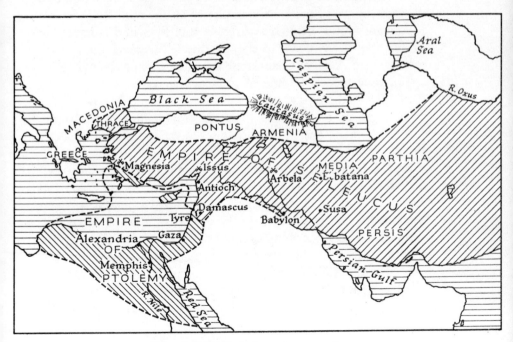

The rival Hellenistic empires 300–64 BC

I   THE EARLY EMPIRES

1   Geography, climate and early inhabitants

THE HISTORY OF EVERY COUNTRY is intimately bound up with its climate, but in Syria, Lebanon and Jordan climatic conditions have been even more important than is usually the case.

The Mediterranean is a rough parallelogram, the long sides running east and west, the short sides north and south. Spain closes the western end of the inland sea and the coast of Syria and Palestine the eastern end. The greater part of the rain which falls in the Mediterranean area comes from the Atlantic Ocean. Such as misses the mountains of Spain, Italy or Greece on the north or the Atlas Mountains on the south, strikes the coast of Syria and Palestine. In summer rain rarely if ever reaches the eastern Mediterranean and the months from April to October are normally completely dry.

The geographical features of Syria and Palestine run north and south. Firstly the coastal plain, then a range of mountains called – from north to south – the Amanus Mountains, the Lebanon, Galilee, Samaria and Judaea, fading out on to the plain of Beersheba.

East of this range, and immediately parallel to it, lies a long deep rift which begins in the Orontes valley, (in Arabic Al Aasi) and continues south of Homs as the Baqa. It then becomes deeper and contains the Sea of Galilee, the River Jordan and the Dead Sea, eventually joining the Red Sea as the Gulf of Aqaba. At the Dead Sea, the valley is 1290 feet below sea level.

Further east again is another range of mountains, likewise running north to south. It begins just south of Homs, where it is called Anti-Lebanon and includes Mount Hermon. Continuing south-

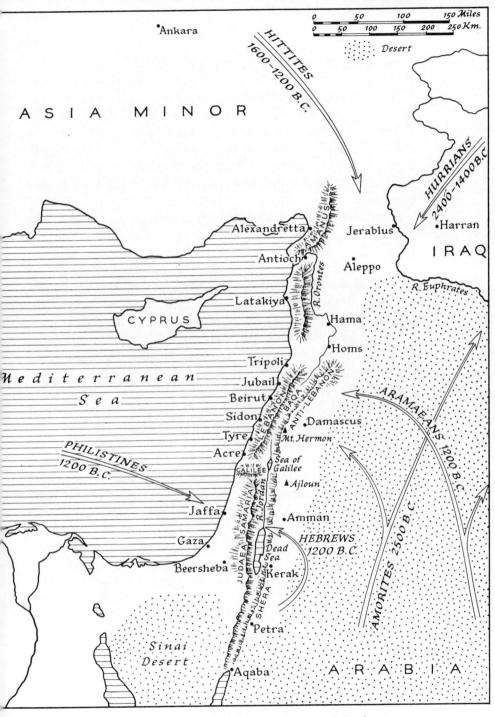

Ankara

HITTITES 1600–1200 B.C.

50 100 150 Miles
50 100 150 200 250 Km.

Desert

ASIA MINOR

HURRIANS 2400–1400 B.C.

Alexandretta

Jerablus

•Harran

Antioch

Aleppo

IRAQ

R. Euphrates

Latakiya

CYPRUS

Hama

R. Orontes

Homs

Mediterranean Sea

Tripoli

Jubail

Beirut

ANTI-LEBANON

BAQA

LEBANON

ARAMAEANS 1200 B.C.

Sidon

Damascus

Tyre

▲ Mt. Hermon

Acre

Sea of Galilee

GALILEE

PHILISTINES 1200 B.C.

▲ Ajloun

R. Jordan

SAMARIA

Jaffa

•Amman

HEBREWS 1200 B.C.

Gaza

Dead Sea

JUDAEA

AMORITES 2500 B.C.

Beersheba

•Kerak

SHERA

Sinai Desert

•Petra

ARABIA

•Aqaba

   II   *Syria as a causeway between the sea and the desert*

wards, it is known as Jebel Ajloun – the Biblical Gilead – and then Kerak and the Shera, the Moab and Edom of the Old Testament.

As the clouds blow in from the west in winter, they strike the first range of mountains, those extending from the Amanus through Lebanon to Judaea. The western slopes of these mountains, with the coastal plain at their feet, receive in general a good water supply during the winter months. Forests and orchards clothe the slopes, fields of wheat and barley, vineyards and orange and olive groves, the plains.

Clouds blown across from the tops of these mountains strike the second range, which extends from the Anti-Lebanon to southern Jordan. Little rain falls on the eastern slopes of the coastal range or on the Jordan valley, but the western-facing slopes of the second range receive a fair rainfall, and are likewise clothed in forests and orchards. Further east, however, the land slopes away from the mountain tops in a gently falling plateau until it peters out in open steppe country, which gradually changes into desert. The cultivation of wheat and barley comes to an end some thirty miles east of the ridge of the second range of mountains and thereafter the steppes are used only for grazing.

This natural division of the country into strips running north and south has divided the population into similar groups. Along the coastal plain of the Mediterranean, the rainfall is adequate and the climate mild and enjoyable. But this long narrow strip of country is shut in on the east by a double range of mountains with the desert beyond them. To these dwellers on the coast, the sea has normally appeared a less formidable obstacle than the mountains and deserts of the interior.

Traffic across the eastern Mediterranean between this coastal plain and Europe has moved in both directions. In Old Testament times, the Philistines were invaders who came across the sea, probably from Greece, and settled on the coastal plain of Palestine. Later the Greeks arrived under Alexander the Great and after them the Romans. Movement across the sea went on even more actively in the opposite direction. The inhabitants of the coastal plain from Acre to Tripoli, called in antiquity the Phoenicians, but whom we call Lebanese, were some of the most daring sailors of the ancient world, who established colonies all round the Mediterranean and as far west as Britain.

While the population of the coastal plains was mixed with European stock and looked across the sea to the west for a livelihood, the inhabitants of the first mountain range – Lebanon to Judaea – were hardy shepherds and farmers, to a large extent tribally organized, sometimes trading with, at other times raiding, the more civilized inhabitants of the coastal plain. The peoples who lived on the eastern mountains were likewise tribesmen, farmers and shepherds, though more martial than those of the Western range, owing to the constant warfare which they were obliged to maintain with the nomadic tribes of the desert.

Movement through the mountains was difficult and dangerous, but just beyond the eastern range the country consisted of open plains, cultivated with grain crops and offering free movement for travellers and commercial caravans. This north to south strip was only some thirty miles wide, between the mountains and the desert. Here, extending from north to south, sprang up a line of cities – Aleppo (the classical Beroea), Homs, Hama, Damascus and Amman.

Thus the cities of Syro-Palestine were marshalled in two lines, as usual running north and south. On the coast Alexandretta, Antioch, Latakiya, Tripoli, Jubail (in early times called Byblos), Beirut, Sidon, Tyre, Acre, Jaffa and Gaza. There were few cities in the two ranges of mountains but between the eastern range and the desert lay Aleppo, Homs, Hama, Damascus, Amman and Petra.

The intervention of the mountains thus divided the cities and thence the cultures of Syro-Palestine into two groups. The Mediterranean coastal group, half Semitic and half European, and the eastern, inland group, preponderantly Semitic, especially in the south.

A few miles east of the inland line of cities, the Syrian desert extends for some four hundred miles to the Euphrates, but tapers to an apex in the north in the vicinity of Aleppo. It consists of rolling steppes, mostly on limestone (not sand), but the rainfall, blocked by the two mountain ranges of Syria and Palestine, is inadequate for agriculture.

When, however, in winter or spring, an exceptionally heavy rainstorm is blown across both mountain ranges, it crosses the Syrian desert to the Euphrates. The course of its passage becomes visible within a few days by the appearance of grass and wild flowers. For a few weeks in spring, the valleys of the desert are carpeted with green. Then the clouds vanish, the sun beats down, the grass fades and the rolling steppes assume a pale fawn colour, shimmering in the noonday heat.

The precarious nature of the rainstorms, however, obliges stockbreeders to lead a nomadic life in tents, moving their camps here and there wherever the accidents of the rainstorms happen to have produced grazing.

From time immemorial, the governments of the cities and the settled areas found it almost impossible to control these bedouins, who spent much of their time in wars between one another or in raiding the villages on the edge of the cultivated area. Periodically the nomads would move into the settled country, either by conquest or by infiltration, and would then become farmers or townsmen.

We find, therefore, that we have parallel belts of population, running north and south. Along the coast were wealthy communities, partly engaged in agriculture but also consisting of merchants and sailors engaged in overseas trade. This coastal population was of mixed origin, consisting largely of immigrants from other Mediterranean countries.

The next group consisted of farmers, shepherds and a few small market towns in the two ranges of mountains. These were partly mixed with the coastal population and partly with the nomads who had infiltrated from the desert.

The next group, sandwiched in between the mountains and the desert, was a line of cities extending from Aleppo in the north to Petra in the south. Then, further east again, came the bedouins of the desert, most of whom had originally come from the Arabian Peninsula. These – the original Arabs – were of racial origin markedly different from that of the coastal population.

The desert has often been aptly compared to a sea and the camel to a ship. The camel, the only means of desert transport until the twentieth century, cannot live in the settled area. As a result, the townsmen and villagers of Syria were unable to move in the desert. More important still, neither armies nor trade could cross it. The desert shut in Syria and Palestine on the east even more effectively than did the Mediterranean on the west.

Syria may, therefore, be thought of as a long narrow strip of land between two seas, the Mediterranean and the desert. As such it was the only land thoroughfare joining Asia and Europe to Africa, as the Isthmus of Panama joins North and South America. This Syro-Palestine causeway was five hundred miles long but only some seventy-five miles wide. Its long 'coastline' was exposed to pirate raids: on the west by sea-pirates, on the east by desert pirates. In these contests, the pirates always enjoyed the advantage of surprise. Appearing unexpectedly off the coast or out of the immensity of the desert, they could plunder towns and villages before the army of the local ruler could assemble, and disappear once more over the horizon, where the Syrians would be unable to follow. Sometimes, however, they remained as conquerors and became integrated into the native population.

The fact that Syro-Palestine was a long isthmus of land between the sea and the desert made it one of the greatest highways of the ancient world. Moreover, this narrow causeway connected several great powers, which included the earliest civilized communities of which we know. To the east, the rich alluvial valleys of the Tigris and Euphrates maintained large populations and wealthy states. To the southwest, the valley and delta of the Nile produced an equally dense population and prosperous governments.

To the north and northwest, from the Caucasus to Greece, an adequate rainfall had sufficed to give birth to powerful nations since before the dawn of recorded history. Syro-Palestine, however, a long narrow strip of country with a precarious and inadequate rainfall, was never able to support a population capable of facing on equal terms its more powerful neighbours in Iraq, Asia Minor or Egypt.

Consequently, like the Low Countries between France and Germany, Syria found herself repeatedly the cockpit in which her more powerful neighbours fought out their rivalries.

These geographical factors account for almost the whole of Syro-Palestinian history. Endless invasions and conquests from north and south and from sea and desert condemned the Syrian causeway-land to repeated catastrophes and desolations. But this stormy history also enabled Syria to play an immensely important role in human development.

Each invading army brought with it a new culture which mingled with those which had already taken root. Every commercial caravan which passed down to Egypt or up to Asia Minor or Iraq, introduced to Syria new commodities, new languages and new ideas. Syria thus became the meeting place of nations, the crossroads of migrating peoples, the exchange and mart of ideas and civilizations. Moreover, the fact that their own ethnic origins were extremely mixed enabled the Syro-Palestinians the more readily to absorb and to pass on to others the many and varied cultural streams which poured into their country.

This has been the vitally important role played by Syria throughout history, from the first dawn of historical records, some three thousand years before Christ, to this very day and hour in which we live. For the remainder of this chapter we will trace, as far as surviving records permit, the means by which this process was carried out in the earliest semi-historical ages.

About 3500 BC a highly civilized people known as the Sumerians dominated Syria and Iraq. Their principal habitat was lower Iraq (between Baghdad and the Persian Gulf to use modern names), but it now appears that they also spread across Syria to the Mediterranean. Their origin is unknown but they were not Semitic. They appear to have been the first originators of picture-writing.

Some time before 2500 BC, the first Semites appear in Syria. They were the Amorites, who may have been nomads from Central Arabia. They defeated the more civilized Sumerians and imposed on them their Semitic language, though Sumerian remained as a learned language for several centuries. The Amorites were taught reading, writing and agriculture by the Sumerians.

In 2450 BC, Sargon I, King of Babylon, conquered Syria, defeating the Amorites, but the conquest was short-lived and the Amorites continued to dominate Syria east of the Lebanon. The Babylonians at this time appear to have been the product of a fusion between the Sumerians and Semitic invaders from Arabia.

With effect from about the same time, perhaps 2400 BC, the Egyptians seem to have dominated the coastal plain of what we call Palestine and Lebanon, thus settling a pattern to be followed for thousands of years, namely, the partition of Syro-Palestine between the great rivals, Egypt and Iraq.

About 1600 BC, the name of Canaanites appears on the coastal plain. These people may not have been one race. Although modern students may be interested in ethnic origins, people were not concerned with such things four thousand years ago. Then, as now in popular parlance, national names were normally based on geography. Canaanites may have thus been a general term for persons living in the Syro-Palestine area, irrespective of racial origins.

The Canaanites, as such, never formed a great state, nor were they conquerors. On the contrary, they devoted themselves largely to trade, paying tribute to powerful invaders when necessary. The language they spoke was Semitic, or, as we should say, akin to Arabic. They were, however, skilled metal-workers, first in copper and bronze and then in iron and perhaps steel, a fact which makes it probable that they came from the north. Infiltrators from the desert could not possibly be metal-workers. They are further alleged to have introduced horses and chariots to Syria, again precluding a desert origin. In brief, the Canaanites seem to have been typical Syro-Palestinians, a mixture of many races and civilizations.

If the Canaanites were indeed invaders from outside, they did not of course replace the original inhabitants. They merely added another strain and a new name to the already mixed population. The Hyksos or so-called Shepherd Kings who conquered Egypt were possibly Canaanites. If this be correct, they were not primitive invaders, as the term Shepherd Kings seems to suggest, but possessed a number of skills unknown to the Egyptians, such as the working of bronze and iron. They were also in advance of the Egyptians in mathematics and science.

The Hyksos conquered Egypt in *c.* 1730 BC. At one time, they seem for a brief period to have united Syria and Egypt into one empire but the two countries then again fell apart. The Egyptian reaction against Hyksos rule came in 1580 BC after a century and a half. They were driven out of Egypt but established themselves in Palestine for a further 130 years. Thutmosis III, who died in 1447 BC, was a Pharaoh who proved to be the Napoleon of his time. He invaded Palestine and Syria, completely defeated the Hyksos and destroyed all their monuments. The Hebrew Exodus from Egypt, recorded in the Old Testament, does not appear to have occurred until *c.* 1250 BC, three centuries after the end of Hyksos rule, though some scholars place it nearly two centuries earlier.

A people known as the Hurrians had infiltrated into Syria perhaps as early as 2400 BC. They were non-Semitic and had apparently come from the north. Some may have become integrated into the Hyksos. Perhaps *c.* 1500 BC, while the Hyksos were being driven from Egypt, the Hurrians or Horites succeeded in forming a powerful state of their own in northern Syria, extending from the Mediterranean to the site of the modern town of Kirkuk in Iraq.

The Hittites, a non-Semitic people, whose real name was Khatti, had long been established in Asia Minor around Ankara, the modern capital of Turkey. About 2000 BC they seem to have been attacked by Indo-European invaders. In 1595 BC, the Hittites attacked Aleppo. In *c.* 1450 BC they conquered all Syria. From 1380 to 1355 BC, they held all Syria and Palestine and were the most powerful state in western Asia.

They clashed with the Egyptians but in 1272 BC a peace was signed between them and Egypt, according to which Lebanon and Syria belonged to the Hittites but Palestine submitted to Egypt. Southern Palestine, nevertheless, seems to have been full of Hittites, as early as the times of the Patriarchs.[1]

The typical Hittite features were distinguished by the large, thick nose, which in Europe and America is believed to be a charac-

20

teristic of the Jews. In fact, however, the Hittites were not Semitic at all. The same type of features are still often to be seen in Syria in both Arabs and Armenians.

The mountains of Lebanon and their northern and southern con-tinuations have throughout history constituted a formidable barrier, shutting off the coastal plain from the interior. In *c.* 1400 B C, we first hear of one of the most famous peoples of antiquity, the Phoeni-cians. Unfortunately the name gives no clue to their racial origin. It was not the name by which they called themselves, but was used by the Greeks to describe them. The word Phoenician is said to be derived from the Greek word for purple and to refer to the purple dye for which Tyre was long famous.

A glance at the map shows that access to the coastal plains from the east was difficult, necessitating the crossing of two parallel ranges of mountains. It would be particularly difficult to nomadic invaders from the desert, whose pack animals and large flocks obliged them to live in the plains.

On the other hand, conquest of the Phoenician coastal plains would be easiest to invaders from the north, who would follow the coast from Asia Minor. Thus it is tempting to imagine that the Hittites must have been densely concentrated in Phoenicia. More-over, the ease with which the Phoenicians (and their descendants the Lebanese) have always mingled with the peoples of Europe, might be held to indicate their Indo-European origin. On the other hand, the Phoenicians spoke a Semitic language. Doubtless, like all the other peoples of the Syrian causeway, they were of part-European and part-Semitic origin.

From *c.* 1300 B C onwards, the Phoenicians proved themselves remarkable sailors and colonizers. Their principal export to Egypt was timber, which is almost non-existent in the Nile valley. Soon, however, they established trading settlements in Cyprus, in Crete, in Greece, in Sicily and in Sardinia. By 1000 B C, the Phoenicians were in Cadiz, Spain, and in North Africa, even, it is believed, in Britain. Carthage, the most famous of Phoenician colonies, was founded *c.* 850 B C.

A thousand years before Christ, civilization was centred in the eastern Mediterranean. In the course of their trading ventures over- seas and their establishment of colonies, the Phoenicians carried the civilization of the East to North Africa and Europe. Most sensational of all their exports, however, was the first alphabet. They are believed to have been the first people to use letters producing sounds, as opposed to the earlier picture-writing. About 800 B C, the Phoenician alphabet was adopted by the Greeks and became the basis of European writing. Simultaneously the Aramaeans adapted it to write their language, through which it developed into the Arabic script, later used for the Koran.

The Phoenicians also discovered the Cape of Good Hope. Sub- sidized by Pharaoh Necho, who reigned from 609 to 593 B C, they started from the Red Sea, rounded the Cape of Good Hope and entered the Mediterranean through the Straits of Gibraltar three years later. Two thousand years were to elapse before the feat was repeated by Vasco da Gama in the opposite direction.

We have departed from strict chronological order to record the navigational exploits of the Phoenicians, and must now return to Syria in the thirteenth century before Christ, where we left the Hittites occupying the dominating position. When the Hebrews, escaping from Egypt c. 1250 B C, invaded Palestine from the east, the Hittites were already in decline and had broken up into many small states. The first tribes encountered by the Hebrews, east of the Dead Sea and the River Jordan, were Amorites, who were Semites, or as we should say, Arabs. As soon as they crossed the Jordan, however, the people seem to have been predominantly non-Semitic, Hittites, Perizzites, Hivites and Jebusites. Jericho, the first 'city' captured, covered an area of only six acres and had walls twenty-one feet high. Such were the great cities fenced up to heaven which stood in the path of the invading Hebrews. The slow conquest and integration of the Children of Israel in Palestine took some 250 years, during which they intermarried freely with the indigenous population.

While the Hebrews were invading Palestine from the east, the Philistines, a seafaring race from Greece, were landing on the coastal

22

plain. By *c.* 1050 BC the Philistines had conquered all the coastal plain of Palestine and reached the foothills, while the Hebrews had gained the leadership in the hill country. From *c.* 1050 to 1000 BC, the Philistines held the upper hand and even garrisoned Bethlehem on the crest of the mountains of Judah and Beisan in the Jordan valley.

The Hebrews and the other hill tribes were still primitive, while the Philistines were skilled metal-workers in copper, brass, bronze and iron. They occupied all the plain country by using iron chariots but the Israelites succeeded in holding on to the hills where wheeled chariots could not operate. The Psalmist's exclamation: 'I will lift up mine eyes unto the hills from whence cometh my strength', must have been a cry from the heart during the century-long struggle with the Philistines.

Some time before 1200 BC, a new wave of Semitic invaders called the Aramaeans had begun to arrive from Central Arabia and had first reached the Euphrates and then northern and eastern Syria. By 1200 BC, they had established their control over Damascus. Like all nomadic invaders, whose strength lies in cohesion and mobility, they were doubtless far less numerous and less civilized than the inhabitants of Syria. But although the Aramaeans acquired their culture from the Syrians, they imposed their language, Aramaic, which was eventually to become the lingua franca of Syria and Palestine and was the language used by Jesus.

Such minor invaders as the Philistines, the Hebrews and the Aramaeans were only able to impose their control in Syria and Palestine because the governments of Egypt and Iraq were in confusion from *c.* 1200 to 900 BC. The Aramaean kings of Damascus were frequently at enmity with Israel. King David, however, who ruled Israel from *c.* 1004 to 960 BC, defeated them and even for a brief period held Damascus, though he never quite subjugated the coastal plain. 'Palestine', says George Adam Smith in his *Historical Geography of the Holy Land*, 'has never belonged to one nation and probably never will', a prophecy which is still true. In the reign of Solomon, who died *c.* 925 BC, the kings of Damascus regained the upper hand.

The Hebrews were, on the whole, backward in art and commerce, their pre-eminence lying in the fields of religion and religious literature. The Ten Commandments were probably the highest moral law known to mankind before the coming of Christ. They went beyond action to thought, requiring love of God and honour to parents and forbidding covetousness. Most primitive religions aimed to propitiate the gods with gifts and worship but little emphasis was laid on morality for its own sake. Hebrew religion, on the other hand, always had an ethical side.

The Assyrians first made their appearance in Syria in 1094 B C. With their capital at Nineveh, near modern Mosul on the Tigris, they were a people of mixed origin, consisting partly of old indigenous races, then of Sumerians from the east, followed by Semites from Arabia and ultimately mixed with the Hurrians from the direction of northern Persia. In 1094 B C, Tiglath-Pileser I conquered all Syria. Soon afterwards, however, the Assyrians disappeared, owing to troubles at home, and were only to return some two centuries later.

During the period from 2500 to 850 B C, the successive invaders of Syria and Palestine had come as migrating nations in search of a new land in which to live. Having defeated the indigenous people of the land, they at first became a ruling class, dominating the country and giving their names and possibly their language to the state which they set up. Gradually they would settle down and become mingled with the former populations. The new integrated state, however, would assume the name of the last conquerors, although the latter were doubtless far fewer in numbers than the conquered. We must not, therefore, imagine that, for example, when the Aramaeans conquered Syria, the Hittites, the Hurrians or the Canaanites ceased to exist. On the contrary, they doubtless remained the largest element in the population, although their defeat had caused their name to be replaced by that of the new conquerors.

In the third verse of the sixteenth chapter of his book, the Prophet Ezekiel denounces with perfect accuracy the mixed origins of the Palestinians. 'Thy father was an Amorite and thy mother an

Hittite', he cries, and the remark would be true of all Syrians. The Amorites, as we have seen, were Semites or 'Arabs', while the Hittites were possibly Indo-Europeans. It is precisely this mixed parentage which has throughout history made Syria a bridge and a clearing-house between East and West.

KEY DATES

	BC	
	c. 3500	Non-Semitic Sumerians dominate Iraq and North Syria
	c. 2500	Appearance of the Semitic Amorites
	2400	Appearance of Egyptians on the coasts of Palestine
	2000	Domination of the coastal areas by Canaanites
	1730	Conquest of Egypt by the Hyksos
	1580	Eviction of the Hyksos from Egypt
	1500	Domination of northern Syria by the Hurrians
	1380	Domination of Syro-Palestine by the Hittites
	1400–800	Phoenician maritime colonization
	1250	Exodus of the Hebrews from Egypt
	1200	Invasion of Syria by the Semitic Aramaeans
	1050	Philistines conquer Palestine coastal plain
	1004–960	Kingdom of David

2 The early empires: Assyria to the Roman Republic

IN THE PREVIOUS CHAPTER we saw Syria and Palestine invaded by successive migrating nations, some Semitic or 'Arab', others non-Semitic. These people were in search of a new land in which to live and soon became integrated with the various other races which had preceded them.

From *c.* 860 B C onwards, however, a change takes place. Invasions become increasingly frequent but they are no longer caused by migrating peoples but by the armies of great powers, established in countries richer and stronger than Syria or Palestine. The object of these invaders was not to seek a new national home for themselves but to extend their rule over subject nations.

Shalmaneser III, the King of Assyria, reigned from 859 to 824 B C. (It is unfortunate that the names Assyria and Syria sound so much alike in English, for they are entirely different words.) In 853 B C, Shalmaneser III defeated an army composed of Aramaeans, assisted by Ahab, King of Israel, on the River Orontes. By 842, all Syria, even including Tyre and Sidon, had been conquered by Assyria. Jehu, King of Israel, who had seized power from Ahab's son by a military *coup d'état* of the usual type, submitted and paid tribute to Assyria.

The Assyrian Empire was one of the first known to us which attempted to organize and administer its conquered territories. The empire fell into a certain confusion *c.* 800 B C, but was re-invigorated by Tiglath-Pileser III in 745 to 727 B C. He was succeeded by his son Shalmaneser V, who reconquered the coastal fortresses of Tyre and Sidon which had been lost. Sargon II, who followed him on the throne, carried Israel away captive to Assyria in 721 B C.

The famous Sennacherib looked beyond Syria and Palestine to the conquest of Egypt, which was finally achieved by Ashur-bani-pal, who reigned from 668 to 626 B C. In spite of this military success, however, Ashur-bani-pal was not a dedicated soldier like his predecessors. He preferred scholarship to war and collected a large library in Nineveh. The Assyrian Empire had lasted 230 years and was rapidly weakening. Meanwhile a new power had appeared in lower Iraq with its capital at Babylon. These people, also called the Chaldaeans, allied themselves with the Medes from northern Persia to resist Assyria. In 612 B C, Nineveh was captured and the Assyrian Empire came to an end.

The confusion in the north encouraged the King of Egypt, Pharaoh Necho, to intervene. Sweeping across Palestine with a great army, he defeated and killed Josiah, King of Judah, at Megiddo and marched on to the Euphrates. In 605 B C, however, Nebuchadnezzar of Babylon completely destroyed the Egyptian army under Pharaoh Necho at Carchemish (the modern Jerablus) and established the undisputed supremacy of Babylon over Syria. In 597 B C, Nebuchadnezzar took Jerusalem. A few years later, however, the King of Judah, relying on assistance from Egypt, rebelled against Babylon. In 586 B C, Jerusalem was re-captured by the Chaldaeans and was razed to the ground.

The Chaldaean Empire had now completely replaced that of Assyria. Israel, Judah and the Aramaean kingdom of Damascus had ceased to exist, and Nebuchadnezzar had conquered Egypt also. The Chaldaean Empire, however, was to prove shortlived. A new and forceful nation had arisen in the east as a result of the fusion of the Medes and the Persians. In 538 B C, Cyrus, King of Persia, finally took the citadel of Babylon and with it the whole Chaldaean Empire. Syria and Palestine, without any attempt at resistance, became provinces of the empire of Persia.

The historical commencement of genuine administrative empires may perhaps be dated from c. 850 B C, when Shalmaneser III conquered Syria. It is true that there had been fleeting occupations in previous centuries by Egypt, Babylon and Assyria, but these appear to have been shortlived and to have merited the name of conquests rather than of empire.

In recent years the word empire has acquired an evil significance, but we must remember that, throughout history, empires have been one of the principal means of spreading civilization. Assyro-Babylonian culture reached Syria through military conquest, passed on thence to Egypt and was carried to Greece and Europe by the Phoenicians. The plough and the wheel, for example, are thought to have been invented by the Babylonians and introduced by them to Syria and Egypt. The Syrians learned from the Babylonians the division of the year into twelve months and the week into seven days. They also called the first day of the week Sunday and the second Moonday. Even we have profited from the knowledge spread by their conquests. It is fascinating to observe the gradual progress in humanity and efficiency achieved by successive empires. The Assyrians were notoriously cruel but Cyrus was modest and humane, and was described by his fellow-citizens as the father of his country.

Cyrus was succeeded by his son Cambyses who, in 525 BC, added Egypt to his dominions which now stretched from the Jaxartes to the Nile delta and from the Black Sea to the Persian Gulf, an empire considerably greater than any of its predecessors. Cambyses died in 521 BC and was succeeded, after three years of civil war, by his cousin Darius, under whom the Persian Empire was extended by the conquest of Thrace and the submission of Macedonia on the west, and by the annexation of the Punjab and Sind in India on the east. Syria and Palestine were but small provinces in the heart of this vast empire which included almost the whole civilized world of that time except China.

The administrative organization introduced by Darius the Great, however, has won him more enduring fame than his military campaigns. He divided the empire into governorships or satrapies, of which at one time there were twenty-eight, Syria and Palestine together forming one of them. Each satrapy reported direct to the capital, Susa, the modern Shush, in southwest Persia. Another innovation was the appointment of three officers to each satrapy – the satrap himself, a military commandant of troops, and a civil secretary. Each of these officers was entitled to write direct to the king, whereby each could be used as a check upon the others.

Under Darius the Great, Aramaic became the official language for inter-provincial communications between the western provinces. Roads were built, taxes were efficiently collected and postal services were rapid. Under the Persians, Syria and Palestine enjoyed two hundred years of stability and prosperity, which must have been an immense improvement on the preceding stormy centuries when they were the cockpit between rival military kingdoms. Phoenician over-seas trade was also extremely prosperous. Damascus was the capital of Syria during the Persian period.

After the death of Darius the Great in 485 B C, the succession of a number of weak kings gave rise to sporadic rebellions and reduced the prestige of the empire. Yet the territories conquered by Darius were still intact 150 years later when Artaxerxes III was assassinated in 336 B C. After a further series of assassinations, Darius III Codomannus ascended the throne.

The adulation which has been lavished on Greece and Rome during the last four centuries in the West has obscured the achieve-ments of the other great races of history. The Persians among others, having been so unfortunate as to be the enemies of the Greeks, have been represented as base oriental slaves. In fact, courage, virility, generosity and energy were the virtues most admired among them. To ride, to shoot, and always to speak the truth were the manly virtues inculcated into their youths. We have seen that they were also efficient administrators and that, compared at least with their Assyrian and Babylonian predecessors, they were in general humane and protected the interests of minorities.

When the Persian Empire first rose to pre-eminence from 538 B C onwards, the Greeks were still learning civilization from the East. A hundred years later, the process was reversed. The Greeks have always been gifted with extraordinary intellectual powers but the subtlety of their minds has often given rise to bitter disputes among themselves. From 450 BC onwards, an extraordinary outburst of energy took place among them. This period of expansion resulted in the arrival of great numbers of Greek merchants and Greek ships on the sea-coasts of Syria. A hundred years before the rise of Alexander, communities of Greek businessmen were already established in all the ports of Phoenicia, bringing with them new ideas, new openings for trade and new knowledge. As the Persian Empire grew weaker, the bustling energy of the Greeks slowly gained ground.

This penetration of Greek thought into Syria was to smooth the way for Greek rule, which, however, could not be realized as long as the many Greek city-states were engaged in constant wars against one another. In 336 BC, however, Philip, King of Macedon, succeeded in persuading the greater part of Greece to accept him as commander-in-chief of the armies of all the Greek states. Philip was murdered almost immediately after this event and was succeeded by his son Alexander. The new ruler, although a Macedonian, had been the pupil of Aristotle and was saturated with Greek thought and Greek culture, which he longed to extend to all the peoples of the world.

The title of the greatest soldier the world has ever seen, which has been lavishly bestowed upon Alexander, is one not easy to award. There can, however, be no doubt that he was altogether a splendid young man, a born leader, gifted with boundless energy, a winning personality, with great mental powers and with that touch of romance which fires the imagination of men. But we may also remember that Greek expansion had begun a century earlier and needed only a heroic leader in order to establish Greek pre-eminence over the civilized world.

Alexander left Macedon in 334 BC. In 333, he defeated Darius III at Issus, on the Gulf of Alexandretta, on the northern border of Syria. Darius fled eastwards to Persia but the Persian fleet, based largely on the harbours of Phoenicia, still commanded the Medi-terranean and was thus in a position to threaten Alexander's com-munications with Greece. As he possessed no fleet capable of challenging the Persians at sea, he decided to eliminate the Persian fleet by capturing all the harbours of the eastern Mediterranean. For this purpose, instead of pursuing Darius, he marched down the Phoenician coast. Tyre resisted for seven months and Gaza for two. All the other coastal towns surrendered and Alexander swept into Egypt and occupied the country without serious opposition. While there he founded Alexandria, since then one of the great seaport cities of history.

In the spring of 331 B C, Alexander was back at Tyre. Marching to invade Persia, he again defeated Darius III at Arbela, the modern Erbil, forty-five miles southeast of Mosul. In 330 B C, Darius was assassinated and Alexander conquered the whole of Persia as far as the River Indus in modern Pakistan. Returning to Babylon he died in 323 B C at the age of thirty-two.

Alexander had the vision to picture a world commonwealth, uniting all the races of mankind, and inspired and guided by Greek culture. With this object in view, he planted no less than seventy Greek cities and made Greek the language of the greater part of the civilized world. He was neither contemptuous nor vindictive towards the peoples whom he had conquered, encouraged marriages between Greeks and Persians and seemed in many ways to be seeking to introduce customs, half-Greek and half-Persian, which would be acceptable to both. Had Alexander lived until he was sixty years old, his system might have been stabilized over his vast empire extending from Macedonia to India. When he died at thirty-two, however, the whole edifice began to disintegrate. Only his own splendid personality had been holding it together.

It must be remembered, however, that the empire which Alexan-der had conquered was the Persian Empire, within almost exactly the same borders except for the small area occupied by the cities of Greece. The ruling class was changed but the vast majority of the peoples continued as before. In fact the unity and efficiency of the Persian Empire facilitated the task of the Greeks, who were able, as the result of two great battles, Issus and Arbela, to take over the complete organization as a going concern.

The sudden and unexpected death of the young Alexander with-out an heir threw the world into chaos and the generals of his army immediately became rivals for the succession. For some twenty years, everything was in confusion. Then the number of rivals grew less by the elimination of the smaller competitors. The Greek homeland was held by Demetrius, Antigonus was in control of Asia Minor and Syria, Seleucus was ruler of Babylon and the East, and Ptolemy had established himself in Egypt. In 301 B C, however, Seleucus defeated Antigonus in Asia Minor, as a result of which he annexed Syria and Asia Minor to his dominions of Iraq and Persia. Ptolemy, however, was able to add Palestine to Egypt. Seleucus then founded the city of Antioch in northern Syria as his capital, naming it after his father Antiochus. Antioch was to remain the capital of Syria throughout the whole classical period, down to the Arab conquest in A D 636 – a period of nearly a thousand years. Actually the remains of this once great city are no longer in Syria but in Turkey, having been handed over by the French mandatory government in June 1939.

Having added Asia Minor and Syria to his former dominions, Seleucus, now surnamed Nicator, ruled a vast empire extending from Asia Minor to the Oxus and the Indus. Since the beginning of history, Syria, placed in the centre between Babylonia, Egypt, Asia Minor and Greece, had been at the heart and centre of the civilized world, but the infertility of her mountains and her deserts and her precarious rainfall had prevented her from competing in wealth and population with the teeming valleys of the Nile, or the Tigris and the Euphrates. Syria had been always the victim of invasion, never the invader. Under the Seleucids, however, Syria herself became the headquarters of a great empire.

But if, under the Seleucids, Syria for the first time became the centre of an empire, she also reverted to her unhappy role of a disputed causeway. Although both the Seleucids and the Ptolemies were Greeks, they were also bitter rivals. During the reign of Seleucus II Callinicus, which lasted from 246 to 226 B C, Ptolemy Euergetes conquered the whole of Syria and took Antioch, but Antiochus III, surnamed the Great, retrieved the whole empire once again.

To some extent, the Seleucids and the Ptolemies reached a *modus vivendi*. The Seleucids were a land empire, while the Ptolemies specialized in sea power. They held Cyprus, a number of Greek islands and certain Greek cities on the Asian shore of the Aegean. They aspired to naval supremacy in the Aegean and the eastern Mediterranean. Their need of naval bases, however, brought them into conflict with the Seleucids for control of the harbours of Palestine and Phoenicia.

We have already seen that Greek influence had been penetrating western Asia for a hundred years before Alexander. From his invasion of Syria in 333 BC until the beginning of the Muslim conquests in AD 634, Graeco-Latin civilization was to dominate Syria and Palestine for nearly a thousand years. Throughout this period, the great city of Antioch founded by Seleucus I Nicator was to be the principal centre from which Greek culture radiated to western Asia. Large numbers of other Greek cities were founded, however. Seleucus Nicator himself established no less than sixteen Antiochs, nine Seleucias, five Laodiceas – called after his mother – and three Apameas, after his wife Apama.

Although the Greek colonies and Greek names spread all over Syria and Palestine, the thoroughness of this Hellenization varied greatly. North Syria and the coastal plain from Antioch to Gaza became almost completely Greek. Laodicea (now Latiqiya), Berytus (Beirut), Ptolemais (Acre), Jaffa, Gaza and Ascalon were typical Greek cities. East of the Lebanon mountains and of the River Jordan, however, Hellenization was only partial. While Greek was the language of the cities and of the educated classes, the peasants and the tribesmen continued to speak Aramaic.

In general, over the whole Syro-Palestinian area, Greek and Aramaic culture, the West and the East, intermingled to produce new and fertile ideas. The Seleucid court was half Greek, half Asian. The language and the literature were Greek, the despotism of the kings was Persian. Some of the Seleucid princes were sent to be educated in Athens, but their one-man rule, their lavish hospitality and their custom of giving splendid gifts were 'Arab'.

The Seleucid armies showed the same peculiarities. Under Antiochus the Great (223–187 BC) the army consisted of twenty

33

thousand Greeks, who fought in the phalanx, using pikes twenty-one feet long. But the archers and the slingers, also some twenty thousand strong, were Arabs, Kurds and Persians. A further ten thousand Arab bedouins fought as tribal auxiliaries while the army was com-pleted by a unit of Indian elephants. In addition to the court and the army, Syrian cities were full of Greek businessmen, many of them pure Greeks from Greece. The senior posts in the civil service were also held by Greeks. Although the Ptolemies and the Seleucids were perpetual rivals, both dynasties were Greek and ruled by means of Greek officials and Greek soldiers. Both governments made great efforts to attract immigrants to their countries from Greece, thereby adding yet another racial element to the population.

In Antiochus the Great, the Seleucids produced a man of genius, determined to restore the empire of Alexander to its full dimensions. Commencing in 210 BC, in a five-year campaign, he reached the frontiers of India and completely re-established the authority of the Seleucid Empire. In 198 BC, he invaded Palestine, defeated the army of Ptolemy, pursued it to Gaza and was about to invade and annex Egypt, when news from the north caused him to return in his tracks.

The Roman Republic which had been slowly rising to increasing pre-eminence in the West, had, in 211 BC, defeated Carthage, her rival for the supremacy of the western Mediterranean. In 200 BC, the Romans invaded Greece. As a result, Antiochus III abandoned his conquest of Egypt and hastened northwards, hoping to check the further advance of Rome. His operations in Greece were un-successful and, in 189 BC, he was heavily defeated by the Roman army at Magnesia in Asia Minor and was forced back to a frontier east of the Taurus.

Both the Ptolemies and the Seleucids were now degenerating into second-class powers and the fear of Rome hung like a thunder-cloud over western Asia. After Magnesia, the Romans imposed a crushing war indemnity on Antiochus III, from which the Seleu-cids never recovered. He died in 187 BC, two years after his defeat, all his hopes and ambitions disappointed. Thereafter the Seleucids

34

fell into a rapid decline. Syria, during their heyday, had been cultured and wealthy. The population is estimated to have risen to some four million people, with another two million in Palestine.

After the death of Alexander the Great in 323 BC, a small Jewish state in the Judaean hills around Jerusalem had been subject to the Ptolemies. In 198 BC, however, as we have seen, Antiochus the Great had conquered Palestine, driving the Ptolemies back to Egypt. In 169 BC, Antiochus IV Epiphanes invaded Egypt. On his return, he visited Jerusalem, entered the Holy of Holies in the Temple, and removed a number of gold and silver vessels.

In 168 BC, Antiochus IV Epiphanes again invaded Egypt but was obliged to withdraw on receipt of a Roman ultimatum. As a result, however, of continuing tension with Egypt, he decided to place a garrison in Jerusalem. The tiny Jewish state was divided against itself. Some of the Jews had become Hellenized, while others wished rigidly to maintain the Law of Moses. Presumably counting on the support of the former, Antiochus Epiphanes caused the Temple of Jerusalem to be rededicated to Zeus. The Hellenizing Jews, however, were the intellectuals of Jerusalem. The peasants doubtless adhered to the old Semitic customs, and bands of rebels soon appeared in the rocky gorges of the Judaean hills – an ideal terrain for guerrillas. The most famous leader of the Jewish irregulars was Judas Maccabaeus, of a family known as the Hasmonaeans.

The policy of the Roman Republic in western Asia was purely selfish – perhaps we should say unscrupulous. Unwilling at the time to embark on further conquests, yet genuinely afraid of despotic eastern rulers, Rome did all that she could do to disrupt any stable government which might arise in Syria. In pursuance of this policy, the Senate encouraged the Jews in their rebellion against Antiochus Epiphanes but gave them no practical help. In 152 BC, the Romans succeeded in engineering a fourteen-year civil war in Syria by recognizing an imposter, Alexander Balas, as the Seleucid king.

In 138 BC, however, Antiochus VII Sidetes mounted the Seleucid throne and rapidly restored order. In 134 BC, he took Jerusalem, suppressed the Jewish rebellion and appeared to be about to restore the empire, when he was killed in Babylonia. Thereafter Syria descended into chaos. Rival Seleucid princelings, each with a band of followers, fought one another and plundered the country-side. In eastern Syria, Arab chiefs established themselves in Edessa, in the Jezira and in Homs. All Persia and the eastern provinces were lost and Seleucid power was reduced to a small kingdom in northwest Syria.

The collapse of the Seleucid Empire after 125 BC made room for the rise of two small independent governments. The first of these was the Jewish Hasmonaean state, ruled from 135 to 105 BC by John Hyrcanus and then by his brutal successor, Alexander Jannaeus (104–78 BC). The Jewish state, which consisted of Jerusalem and the surrounding Judaean hills, seized the opportunity to annex the coastal plain down to Jaffa (then called Joppa) and to destroy the hated city of Samaria, thirty-five miles north of Jerusalem.

Further east, the Nabataeans had built up another independent state. From very early times, the luxury products of India and China had been in demand on the shores of the eastern Mediterranean. Much of this trade came by sea to Aden or the Yemen, whence it was carried up the eastern shore of the Red Sea by camel. The Nabataeans were an Arab tribe who handled this trade. Their principal commercial depot was at Petra (in modern Jordan) where they had established a wealthy city in almost inaccessible mountains. At Petra the caravan route divided. (See map III, page 43.) One road turned westward to Egypt, a second northwest to Gaza, while a third continued northwards to Damascus.

The Nabataeans first appear in history as merchants in 312 BC, but thereafter they played no part in the struggles between the Ptolemies and the Seleucids. A people entirely devoted to commerce, they were solely preoccupied in escorting their caravans from Aden to Damascus or Egypt. The breakdown in public security resulting from the collapse of the Seleucid Empire obliged them to escort their caravans with military forces and then to build fortified staging posts along the trade routes. Finally, in 85 BC, their King Aretas (in Arabic, Haritha) became lord of Damascus also. The Nabataeans spoke Arabic, not Aramaic. Their language and alphabet were the parents of the Koran.

A further result of the Seleucid collapse had been the rapid rise of Parthia in northern Persia. In 92 B C, Mithridates II, the Parthian king, signed a treaty with Rome, making the upper Euphrates the western boundary of Parthia.

The Roman Republic, however, was itself in confusion. In 133 B C, the Gracchi had started a social revolution, which was followed by a slave rebellion in Sicily, civil war in Italy and endless riots in Rome itself. The Roman polity was profoundly corrupt, bribery and intimidation being widespread. In 88 B C, as the result of wars and confusion in Asia Minor, the Roman commander Sulla arrived with an army. In four years of war, he asserted Roman supremacy in Asia Minor but then returned to Rome, where he made himself military dictator. Syria had not been involved in Sulla's campaigns but Roman power was now immediately north of the frontier.

In 83 B C, however, Tigranes, King of Armenia, overran northern Syria and established his headquarters in Antioch. Nine years later, in 74 B C, a Roman army was again operating in Asia Minor. The feeble heirs of the Seleucids implored the assistance of the Roman commander, Lucullus, to evict Tigranes from Syria. Lucullus drove out the Armenians and appointed a Seleucid princeling to be ruler of Syria with the title of Antiochus VIII.

The anarchy in which the Roman Republic had been involved for sixty years had enabled great numbers of pirates to infest the Mediterranean. Seaborne commerce was arrested and the corn supply of Rome was threatened. The inefficiency and corruption of the Roman government was no longer tolerable. In 71 B C, three army commanders, Pompey, Caesar and Crassus, seized power as a triumvirate.

In 67 B C, Pompey was given *carte blanche* to sweep the Mediterranean of pirates, an operation in which he was successful in the short space of three months, finishing the campaign in Cilicia. This victory marked out Pompey as the man of the hour and, in 66 B C, he was made commander-in-chief in the East with full powers. He began his task of asserting Roman power by making a treaty with Phraates, King of Parthia, the traditional ally of Rome, against

Tigranes, King of Armenia, but when Tigranes sued for peace, Pompey made an alliance with him against his own ally, Phraates. This piece of double-dealing was to lead to disastrous results for Rome and Syria alike. (See map III, page 43.)

Pompey entered Syria in the spring of 64 B C. He found northern Syria divided between Antiochus VIII on the west and a number of Arab chiefs on the east side, along the edge of the desert. Most of Palestine was dominated by the Jewish state while, east of the Jordan, the Nabataean Kingdom extended from south of Petra, up to and including Damascus. Pompey made a comprehensive settle-ment in the East. Most of Asia Minor was divided into Roman provinces. Armenia became a vassal kingdom. Syria was likewise made a province under a Roman governor.

In the south, Pompey took Jerusalem and, like Antiochus Epip-hanes, himself entered the Holy of Holies. He reduced the Jewish state to the hill country of Judaea, and, in 63 B C, placed it under Hyrcanus II of the Hasmonaean family, but in subordination to the Roman pro-consul of Syria, whose capital was Antioch. The Nabataean king, Aretas III, retained Trans-Jordan and Damascus.

In 56 B C, the Roman Triumvirs decided to send Crassus to the East and he arrived in Syria in 54 B C. The Parthians, still resentful at Pompey's treachery, had already begun hostilities. Crassus decided to march across the open plains of the Jezira to the Tigris. After crossing the River Balikh (Latin Balissus) the Romans, as they marched across the plains of the Jezira, were suddenly attacked by a Parthian army. (See map III, page 43.)

The Roman army, which consisted of seven legions, was three times as numerous as the Parthians, who were all cavalry. Refusing to close, the Parthian horse-archers continued all day long to shoot their arrows into the closed ranks of the legions, who had no means of replying. After nightfall, the Romans fled to the shelter of Harran (Latin Carrhae) and then tried to gain the mountainous country to the north, but were intercepted and virtually exterminated, Crassus himself being killed.

Fortunately the resulting invasion of Syria by the Parthians was not commanded by Surenas, the brilliant officer who had destroyed

38

the legions of Crassus. Surenas had been too successful, had incurred the jealousy of his king and had been executed for his popularity. Nevertheless northern Syria was occupied by the Parthians.

While the Parthians were conquering Syria, Rome was again torn by civil war. In January 49 BC, Caesar crossed the Rubicon and war commenced between him and Pompey, who was defeated on 9 August 48 BC at Pharsalus. Pompey escaped to Egypt but was assassinated when he landed at Alexandria. Four years later, on 15 March 44 BC, Caesar himself was assassinated and Rome was plunged into a further series of civil wars. In 42 BC Octavian, Caesar's adopted son, and Mark Antony defeated Brutus and Cassius at Philippi. Mark Antony and Octavian were left at the head of the state.

By agreement with Octavian, Antony went to restore order in the East, where Pacorus, the son of the Parthian king, had taken Jerusalem. In the spring of 36 BC, Antony, to avenge the defeat of Crassus, launched his attack on Parthia but failed to gain a decisive victory and was obliged to retreat with heavy casualties. Meanwhile Antony had lost popularity in Rome owing to his liaison with Cleopatra, the last Greek ruler of Egypt of the family of Ptolemy. At length, on 2 September 31 BC, Antony was defeated at Actium by Octavian who, with the title of Augustus, was to rule alone for forty-three years, from 29 BC to AD 14.

The Roman Republic, like the city-states of Greece, had originated with the government of one town where all the citizens could assemble to discuss public affairs. When Roman rule was extended to all Italy, then to Greece, Spain, Africa and Asia, the machinery proved quite inadequate. The annually appointed consuls were able to act as mayors of their city, but when they became commanders of armies overseas their amateurish operations often led to disaster. Roman governors sent to distant provinces were unpaid and unsupported by trained civil servants, but were often accompanied by business friends from Rome who hastened to Asia to profit by the money-making rackets organized by the governors. The taxes were farmed out to 'publicans', who, in partnership with Roman financiers, drained the life-blood of the conquered nations.

The Roman Republic has been idealized in the West as the model of democracy and justice. The truth was somewhat different. At least, in so far as Syria and Palestine were concerned, the forty or fifty years from 64 BC, the date of Pompey's settlement, until the Augustan reforms began to take effect, were a time of continual disorder, instability and extortion. The abolition of the republic was inevitable if Roman hegemony were to survive.

The first and most essential reform introduced by Augustus in connection with the provinces was the creation of an efficient service of salaried civil officials to carry on the administration. The second was the reform of taxation, based on a series of census operations, making reasonably accurate assessment possible. In most cases, the collection of direct taxes was henceforward carried out by officials, instead of being farmed out to contractors. Moreover an intensive road-building programme made the provinces more accessible and thereby facilitated the closer supervision of the administration. As a result, Syria settled down to the enjoyment of many centuries of the Roman peace.

In Palestine the situation was less happy. Herod the Great had been made King of Judaea by the Romans. Although somewhat arbitrary and ruthless in his exercise of authority, he was active in developing the economic resources of the country. He built on the Mediterranean a new port which he called Caesarea and he began the reconstruction of the Temple of Jerusalem. But being a Hellenizer and a friend of Rome, he was bitterly hated by orthodox Jews.

In the north, Augustus, who preferred diplomacy to force, concluded peace, in 20 BC, with the Parthian king, whom he persuaded to return the Roman eagles captured from Crassus. The boundary of Parthia was again established on the Euphrates. East of the Jordan, the Nabataean Kingdom retained its independence and its hold on Damascus.

In view of his general policy of restraint and moderation, it is curious that Augustus in 25 BC should have launched a military expedition under Aelius Gallus, for the conquest of the Yemen. A force of some ten thousand men set off to move down the Arabian coast of the Red Sea. Marching in extreme heat and often without water, the expedition suffered intensely and was ultimately obliged to turn back without reaching Aden, though, surprisingly enough, it does seem to have reached Marib in the Yemen. The object of the expedition was probably economic. Not only did the Indian trade pass through the Yemen but South Arabia itself produced frankin, cense, myrrh and gold.

KEY DATES

BC

853–842	Assyrian conquest of Syria and Palestine
721	Israel carried away captive
612	Assyrian Empire replaced by the Chaldaean
586	Destruction of Jerusalem by Nebuchadnezzar
538	Destruction of the Chaldaean Empire by Cyrus, King of Persia
334–330	Destruction of the Persian Empire by Alexander the Great
323	Death of Alexander
301	Establishment of the Seleucid Empire in Syria
189	Antiochus the Great defeated by the Romans at Magnesia
64	Pompey's settlement. Syria becomes a Roman province
29	Augustus becomes the first Roman Emperor

3   From Augustus to Muhammad

WITH THE REIGN OF AUGUSTUS, the Roman Republic and
Roman liberty came to an end but a rapid rise in the efficiency of the
administration resulted. In the provinces especially, professional and
disciplined civil servants replaced the corrupt and unscrupulous
politicians of republican days.

The Romans had no rigid system of administration which they
insisted on enforcing all over the empire. On the contrary, they were
willing to take each country as they found it and to use the local
institutions with which the inhabitants were already familiar. Where
they found some tribal chief dominating a certain territory, the
Romans did not attempt to change the system of government to fit
their own political theories. The existing authorities were allowed
to continue to govern in accordance with local custom, as long as
the basic interests of the empire were safeguarded. Thus thoughout
the Roman period, the eastern or Semitic side of the country, Homs,
Damascus and Amman (to use their modern names) continued to
be governed by 'Arab' princes.

The intense hatred of Rome shown by the peoples of Syria and
Judaea in republican times had been almost solely due to the
exorbitant system of taxation. The right to collect taxes was sold by
auction to contractors who were free to extort as much as they could
from the public. The New Testament abounds in references to these
hated 'publicans'. The amount of the taxes, however, at least by
modern standards, had not been heavy and local traditional methods
of assessment were recognized. In Syria, the tax was based on

42

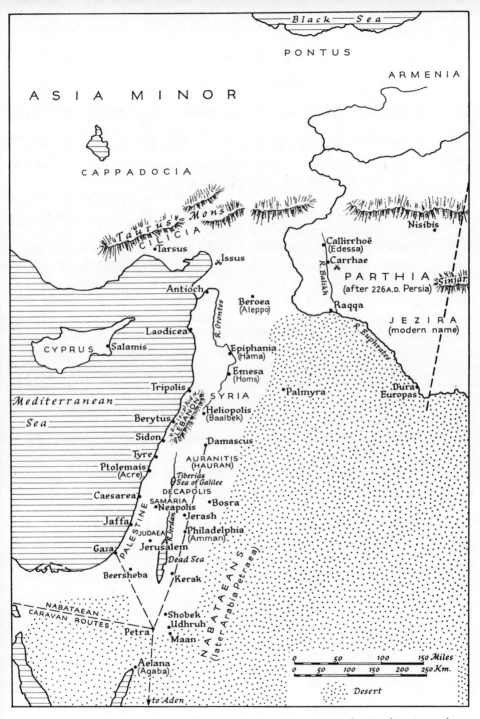

III   *Syria under the Romans. (Note: The Frontier against the Parthians was the River Euphrates but it was later moved east to the line Nisibis to Dura Europas)*

one-tenth of the produce on agricultural land and an animal tax was levied by a count of the numbers of animals. These taxes, which survived until our own times, were probably already traditional when the Romans took them over. In republican days, therefore, it was not the amount of the taxes which had been onerous but the oppressive and extortionate methods of collection.

The army organized by Augustus consisted of two portions, the legions which were composed entirely of Roman citizens, and the auxiliaries, who were recruited from the province itself. The recruit-ment of auxiliaries was a new departure. Under the republic, subject races had not been employed in the armed forces. Service in the auxiliaries was for twenty-five years and the men, when discharged, were awarded Roman citizenship. This was an innovation with profound social implications. In future, ever increasing numbers of Syrians were to obtain Roman citizenship.

In addition to its civilization and the intellectual pre-eminence of its people, Syria was of importance to the empire as the military base of the defence against Persia. The desert being impassable to armies, military operations were confined to the area north of a line drawn from Aleppo to Mosul. Army headquarters were in Antioch and the garrison of Syria under Augustus consisted of four legions, each of 5500 men. An equivalent number of auxiliaries were locally recruited. Syria, Palestine and Jordan are still dotted with places called Lejjoon, the sites of the ancient cantonments of the Legions.

The Roman Empire was based on city life, capitalism and big business. It was therefore natural that the Hellenized cities, parti-cularly on the Mediterranean coast, should enjoy a period of prosperity and influence. Antioch rose to be the third largest city in the empire, conceding pride of place to Rome and Alexandria only. It was famous for its street lighting at night, said to have made the city as bright as day. There was running water in almost every house in Antioch, a convenience which did not become general in Europe until eighteen hundred years later. Daphne, the garden suburb of Antioch, was famous for its amusements, as also for its easy moral standards. 'Antioch yielded with reluctance to the majesty of Rome itself,' says Gibbon in one of his sonorous sentences.

44

Berytus, the modern Beirut, enjoyed the especial favour of Augustus, who improved the harbour and gave the city the status of a colony² for the settlement of army veterans. As a result, Berytus acquired a Roman flavour, most of the other cities remaining primarily Greek.

Berytus was the site of the most famous law school in the Roman East. It is fascinating to observe how the same characteristics are to be distinguished in each locality nearly two thousand years later, for Beirut has become intellectually as prominent in our own times as it was under the Romans.

Augustus also bestowed the title of Roman colonies on Baalbek, on Neapolis (the modern Nablus in Jordan) and on other cities. In Seleucid times, a number of Greek cities had been founded (or older cities had become Hellenized) east of the Jordan and Lebanon, that is to say in the predominantly 'Arab' area. With the Seleucid collapse and the consequent deterioration of public security, ten such cities concluded a league for their mutual defence against the 'Arab' tribes. They called themselves the Decapolis or Ten Cities, of whom those still surviving are Scythopolis (the Arabic Beisan), Jerash, Philadelphia (now Amman, the capital of Jordan) and Bosra, on the southern slopes of the present Jebel Druze. The ruins still visible at Kanawat mark the site of another called Kanatha. All except Beisan were east of the Jordan.

Almost all these Greek cities were of similar design. A paved road-way coming in from the country led to an arched gateway, built of stone. Inside this gate was an open space, sometimes the forum of the city, surrounded by a massive colonnade, which normally looked right up the long, straight main street. This, the principal thoroughfare, was likewise colonnaded on both sides, and was lined by handsome public and private buildings, with richly carved façades. The poorer dwellings and shops were relegated to back streets.

In addition, there were temples with the usual classical colonnaded porticoes, and, in every Greek city, an amphitheatre. Sometimes these great constructions, with their high tiers of seats arranged in a semi-circle for spectators, were built upon flat ground above vaulted

45

chambers. At others, as at Jerash, they were built on the hollow side of a hill. The theatre at Philadelphia (modern Amman) probably held some seven thousand spectators.

It is extremely interesting to note that all inscriptions to gods in the Greek cities of the Decapolis are entirely Greek. In other towns in eastern Syria and Trans-Jordan, contemporary inscriptions to Semitic gods and goddesses have been found, but in the Greek cities of the Decapolis never.

Many men born in the Ten Cities seem to have settled in Rome, even before the reign of Augustus. Philodemus, a poet and Epicurean philosopher, was born in Gadara – now Umm Qeis in northern Jordan, in the first century B C. He moved to Rome, where he was a contemporary of Cicero and was well known for his wit and his profligacy. Cicero, however, praises his philosophical writings and the elegance of his poems.

Another intellectual who early settled in Rome was Theodosius, likewise born in Gadara, who must have achieved a reputation, for he was chosen by Augustus to be tutor to the future emperor, Tiberius.

Syria in Roman times supplied the empire with great numbers of lawyers, doctors, philosophers, sophists and even imperial secretaries. The Syrians were distinguished for their cleverness, quick intellect, and fluency rather, perhaps, than for their profundity. All these characteristics still distinguish them today. In brief, the city populations of Syria had become completely integrated into the Roman community. The retention of the name of Rome may perhaps convey the impression that the empire was controlled by Italians. Such had been the case in republican times but the empire was, in reality, a Mediterranean commonwealth, of which Italy, Greece, Syria and Egypt were the wealthiest and the most civilized members.

Perhaps the greatest blessing conferred upon its citizens by the Roman Empire was its extent. From Britain to the Euphrates and from the German border to the Sahara the same government ruled, the same official language was spoken, the same laws observed. Moreover, the whole area was covered by an ever increasing network of roads, facilitating travel, commerce and control.

We have already seen that, a thousand years before Christ, the Phoenicians had established trading colonies round the Mediterranean and even on the shores of the Atlantic. In Roman Imperial times, Syrian sailors and Syrian merchants were in evidence all over the Mediterranean. Syrian business communities were established in Sicily, in Naples, in Ostia and Rome, in Spain and in France, particularly in Marseilles, up the Rhône valley and in Lyons.

The ease with which the city populations of Syria became integrated into the Roman comity was doubtless due to their mixed racial origin – half Semitic, half Indo-European – and to the three hundred years of Hellenization which had succeeded the conquests of Alexander. The villages, however, were but little affected by the Hellenizing process. With the Roman Empire, Latin became the official language, and Greek the lingua franca of the educated, but the peasants and the tribesmen continued to speak Aramaic.

In the cities, the prominent people were Roman officials and the rich merchants and industrialists. In rural areas, however, particularly in the east, there was an upper class of landowners, village headmen and tribal leaders. Among these people, family discipline and loyalty has remained a persisting force, even down to our own times. Middle-class women, when they went out, were half veiled, though circumcision, a Semitic custom, had in general been abandoned. In one respect Syria was more fortunate than Italy – there were no slaves or serfs on the land.

The segregation of the rural and the city population has, however, persisted to this day and is doubtless due to the frequent influx of foreigners to the cities, whereas the rural and desert populations, especially in the east, were more purely Semitic.

Augustus died in AD 14, leaving a well-administered and peaceful Mediterranean empire, in which an ever-increasing number of persons was achieving the status of Roman citizens, regardless of their racial origins. He was followed by his adopted son, Tiberius, in whose reign occurred, all unperceived by the rich and the great, the most important event in the history of the world, the death of Jesus Christ in Jerusalem.

In AD 66, a general rebellion broke out in the little mountain state of Judaea, and the small Roman garrison of Jerusalem was massacred. The Emperor Nero appointed Vespasian, an experienced com, mander, with three legions to suppress the revolt. Vespasian began with careful thoroughness. In 67, he occupied Galilee, and the next year Samaria and Beersheba, thereby isolating the little Jewish state of Judaea.

At this stage, however, news came of the death of Nero without an heir. Four army commanders, of whom Vespasian was one, attempted to seize the throne. Leaving his son Titus to complete the conquest of Jerusalem, Vespasian left for Italy. In August 70, Jerusalem was taken by assault. The city was sacked, the temple destroyed and the Jewish State came to an end. Judaea remained a Roman province with the Tenth Legion as garrison of Jerusalem.

The Jewish war bequeathed to us one of the most famous and valuable historians of antiquity, the Jew, Flavius Josephus. Born in Jerusalem in 37, he first fought with the Jews against the Romans. Then, changing sides, he became a client of Vespasian and, after the fall of Jerusalem, accompanied Titus to Rome. His *Antiquities of the Jews* and *Wars of the Jews* give a vivid account of the events of his time.

In 106, Trajan, an energetic soldier/emperor, ordered the governor of Syria to abolish the Nabataean Kingdom. A single campaign was sufficient to capture Petra and the Nabataean state, which had lasted for several centuries, became a Roman province with the name of Arabia Petraea. The capital of the province was first located in Petra but was subsequently moved to Bosra, which was also the headquarters of the Third Legion. The Fourth Legion garrisoned the southern half of Trans/Jordan, where they occupied two canton, ments, one at Lejjoon east of Kerak and one at Udhruh, on the road from Shobek to Maan, where extensive ruins still exist. A paved all/weather road was also built from Bosra through

48

Philadelphia (Amman), Kerak, Shobek and Udhruh to Aqaba. A part of the paving is still plainly visible.

The age of the Antonines in the Roman Empire has often been rightly represented as one of the happiest eras ever enjoyed by any nation. The empire was efficiently and benevolently governed by a competent professional civil service, with a philanthropist at its head. Unfortunately Marcus Aurelius died in 180 and was succeeded by the worthless Commodus. The empire had passed its peak. After thirteen years of confusion, Septimius Severus was placed upon the throne by the legions.

When Septimius Severus, then a Roman army officer, had been commanding a legion in Homs in 187, he had married a local lady of the name of Julia Domna. Septimius Severus had himself been born in Leptis, near Tripoli, in North Africa. In 193, Septimius Severus was made emperor and governed with some success until he was killed in Britain in 211. His son, best known as Caracalla, had been borne by Julia Domna at Lyons in France, and was one of the worst emperors who ever wore the purple. He was half Syrian and half North African. Caracalla reigned from 211 to 217, when he was assassinated at Edessa by Macrinus, the Praetorian prefect. Meanwhile the sister of Julia Domna had a daughter who was married to the priest of the sun god of Homs. The post was perhaps hereditary, for their son, Elagabalus, appears to have inherited his father's duties, which consisted in conducting the gorgeous ritual of the sun god. Elagabalus was fourteen years old when his cousin, the Emperor Caracalla, was murdered.

In 218, the Syrian legions suddenly declared for this Syrian boy-priest as emperor. Macrinus was defeated and killed in Antioch, Elagabalus entered Rome in triumph, and the worship of the sun god of Homs was extended all over the empire. Elagabalus' brief reign was marked only by his endless acts of extravagance and debauchery.

After four disgraceful years, Elagabalus was murdered, but so powerful had the Syrians become that he was succeeded unopposed by his cousin, Alexander Severus, a boy of thirteen years, born at

Arqa in Lebanon. Alexander, however, though still a boy, behaved like a wise and honourable man. He reduced taxation, raised the value of the currency and endeavoured to check vice and luxury. He waged a successful war against Persia, for which he celebrated a triumph in Rome in 233. He was, however, unable to restore the discipline of the army and was killed in 235 in a military mutiny in Gaul at the early age of twenty-six.

The accession of Septimius Severus, with his Syrian wife, naturally encouraged Syrian intellectuals to move to Rome. The emperor chose a Syrian called Antipater as his private secretary, and later as tutor to his sons, Caracalla and Geta. Later he raised Antipater to consular rank and made him governor of Bithynia. As his pupil Caracalla was to be one of Rome's worst emperors, the influence of Antipater on his young charge does not seem to have been a success.

One of the most prolific writers of the time was Lucian, a Syrian. No less than eighty-two works have come down to us ostensibly from his pen.[3] His style was satirical and mocks with equal venom at the gods of Olympus and the Romans of his own time. He was appointed procurator of Egypt by the Emperor Commodus.

Porphyry was born in Batanaea in the modern district of Hauran, south of Damascus. He emigrated to Rome, where he wrote many books on philosophy, rhetoric, mathematics and other subjects. He is most famous as a neo-Platonist and a pupil of Plotinus.

Papinian was born in Homs and studied law in Beirut. He was related to Julia Domna, the wife of Septimius Severus, who sum-moned him to Rome as his legal adviser. He was, however, dismissed and executed by order of the infamous Caracalla in 212. The legal code of the Emperor Justinian, drawn up three centuries later, was said to have borrowed extensively from the writings of Papinian. It is noticeable that these and many more Syrian intellectuals who distinguished themselves under the Roman Empire were nearly all educationists, philosophers or lawyers.

In addition to her intellectuals, Syria was known from early

50

imperial days for her entertainers. She was famous for her musicians, flute-players, dancing girls, and circus acrobats. Her girl flute-players were famous in Rome for their charm and easy morals. Juvenal (AD 60–140) complains of the alleged corruption of Roman manners by Syrian players.

The half-Syrian descendants of Septimius Severus had been unfortunate. The discipline of the army had been undermined by the excesses of Commodus, the worthless son of Marcus Aurelius, and was not to be restored until the accession of Claudius in 268. Only eight years after the death of the Syrian Emperor Alexander Severus, another Syrian was to don the purple. Philip had been born in a village near Bosra on the edge of the Syrian desert, and thus may well have been of pure Arab descent.

The young Emperor Gordian, in the course of a campaign against Persia, was murdered on the upper Euphrates and Philip the Arabian, the Praetorian prefect, was hailed as emperor by the soldiers. Philip was not unworthy to rule and conducted several victorious campaigns on the Danube. But he too fell a victim to the indiscipline of the times and was killed in a military mutiny in 249. The long decline had set in. Wars and invasions were rife all over the empire, while rival military commanders fought one another for the purple.

In Syria, the internal troubles of the empire were aggravated by the rise of the Sasanid dynasty. The Parthians, originally nomads from east of the Caspian – half Turkish and half Median perhaps – had reigned for some 350 years. Often harassed by civil wars, dynastic rivalries and nomad invasions from the steppes, the Parthians had little spare time in which to challenge the Romans.

The Sasanids, however, were natives of Fars in west Persia, and claimed to be descended from the dynasty of Cyrus and Darius. The rise of the Sasanids was, therefore, something of a Persian national revival against the domination of the nomads of the northeast. In about 212, Ardashir I challenged the Parthian supremacy. The final battle was fought in 226 on the plain of Hormuz, east of Ahwaz. The Parthians were completely defeated and their King Ardawan was killed.

The new Persian national revival soon proved itself to be aggressive. In 231, Ardashir I invaded northern Syria but was repulsed. His son, Sapor I, captured Nisibin, Harran and then Antioch, but the invasion was ultimately halted in 243.

The Roman Empire at this time seemed to be on the verge of collapse. The Franks and the Allemanni broke through the Roman defence line and invaded Gaul. In 251, the Goths crossed the Danube and defeated and killed the Emperor Decius. Sapor took advantage of the crisis once again to invade Syria, swept across the Euphrates unopposed and occupied Antioch in 258. Not until 260 did a Roman army appear under the aged Emperor Valerian. Sapor was obliged to evacuate Antioch and re-cross the Euphrates but near Edessa the Romans were defeated and Valerian was taken prisoner. The story is well known of how the captured Roman emperor was obliged to accompany Sapor as his slave and to kneel down as a mounting-block whenever the Great King wished to mount his horse.

Shortly afterwards Sapor again invaded Syria, occupied Antioch unopposed, crossed the Taurus Mountains and laid waste eastern Asia Minor with savage barbarity. But his return home was less triumphant than he had expected, owing to the courage of Odena-thus, Prince of Palmyra, a city which merits a brief digression in our narrative.

Before the discovery of America or of the Cape of Good Hope, the world's greatest trade route was that connecting the Indian Ocean with the Mediterranean. Sometimes this oriental trade came by ship from India and up the Red Sea to Egypt. At others, the merchandise was unloaded at Aden and carried by camel caravan to Petra, Egypt or Syria, the trade which had enriched the Nabataeans. A third route lay up the Persian Gulf and thence by caravan up the Euphrates and across the desert to Antioch. In 106, as we have seen, Trajan had destroyed the Nabataeans and had thereby stimulated the Persian Gulf route, which brought wealth and importance to Palmyra. The Palmyrenes became rich merchants by meeting the ships at the head of the Persian Gulf, escorting the caravans and selling the silks, the spices and the luxury goods of the East to the merchants of Antioch. Hadrian had built up Palmyra as a frontier fortress against Parthia but the Palmyrenes, like the Nabataeans before them, had their own troops to protect their convoys.

When Sapor sacked Antioch and laid waste Asia Minor in 262 and 263, Odenathus, the Prince of Palmyra, waited quietly in his oasis, which, surrounded by deserts, was inaccessible to the Persian army. In 263, however, when Sapor attempted to return to Persia, laden with loot and driving gangs of prisoners into slavery, the people of Palmyra took the initiative. Numbers of Arab horse men and camel men poured down upon the long columns of the Persian army, cutting off stragglers, annihilating detachments, recovering convoys of loot and freeing gangs of prisoners. So disorganized did the invaders become that Odenathus was able to capture a number of wives of the Great King himself.

Odenathus even followed the retreating enemy as far as the Sasanid capital of Ctesiphon, on the Tigris, to which for a short time he laid siege. Then, returning home, he occupied Syria and Asia Minor as far west as Ankara, provinces from which the Romans had fled and which had been mercilessly plundered by Sapor. So great was the moral effect of his victory that the Roman Senate conferred upon him the title of Augustus. 'The majesty of Rome', writes Gibbon, 'oppressed by a Persian, was protected by an Arab of Palmyra.' In 266, at the height of his glory, Odenathus was assassinated in Homs.

Odenathus was succeeded by his even more famous widow, the beautiful Zenobia. Well read, a student of history who spoke several languages, the Queen of the East was no less ambitious than her husband. For five years she continued to govern alone, during which time her armies occupied not only all Syria and Palestine but also Egypt.

The period of eighty eight years, lasting from the death of Marcus Aurelius in 180 to that of the dissolute Emperor Gallienus in 268, had been for Rome one of continual defeats and military revolts. In 268, however, the rise of a succession of great and capable emperors suddenly restored the fortunes of the empire. Claudius, in a short reign of two years, utterly defeated the Goths, who had invaded Macedonia. He was succeeded by Aurelian, who, by the restoration of discipline in the army, was able to regain much of the lost prestige of the empire. Aurelian, in 272, decided to restore the imperial authority in Syria.

Zenobia, less prudent than Odenathus, who had conciliated Rome while rendering himself virtually independent, defied the authority of Aurelian. In 272, the soldier-emperor crossed to Asia Minor and marched unopposed to northern Syria. The army of Palmyra gave battle outside Antioch and again near Homs but was then obliged to retire to Palmyra. After a long and difficult siege, the city was taken and Zenobia, after a vain attempt to escape by camel, was carried a prisoner to Rome. In 274, she graced the triumph of Aurelian, led in golden chains in front of his chariot.

The emperor behaved with gallant clemency towards the fallen queen, who was given a villa in which to reside at Tivoli, twenty miles from Rome. Here she is said to have married a Roman noble by whom she raised a second family, and the Queen of the East terminated her life in the safer, if less glamorous, role of a Roman matron.

The revival of the Roman power which had been initiated by Aurelian was maintained by his successors. In 296, Diocletian (284–305) established his headquarters in Antioch for a campaign against Persia. After alternative defeats and victories, the Romans were finally victorious, and peace was signed at Nisibis. As a result of this victorious campaign, Syria enjoyed forty years of peace with Persia.

The death of Diocletian in 305 was followed by twenty years of civil wars which were terminated only in 324 when Constantine became sole emperor, a position which he was to occupy until his death in 337.

Three events which occurred in the reign of Constantine were profoundly to affect the future of Syria. The first was the adoption of Christianity as the official religion of the empire. The second was, in 324, the foundation of Constantinople as a second imperial capital. The third was the division of the empire into three parts between the sons of Constantine. Another Sapor was on the throne of Persia and was encouraged by the death of Constantine to renew hostilities with Rome. The war dragged on inconclusively, the resistance of the fortress of Nisibis preventing Sapor from invading Syria.

On 3 November 361 Constantius, the son of Constantine, died near Tarsus and was succeeded by Julian, a nephew of Constantine. The new emperor had been brought up as a Christian but subsequently endeavoured to re-introduce the ancient gods of Rome. As a result, he has become known as Julian the Apostate. The first task which confronted him was that of putting an end to the Persian war. Julian spent the winter of 361–2 at Antioch, where he annoyed the notoriously lax and frivolous citizens by his solemnity. In the spring, he crossed the Euphrates with an army of 65,000 men.

All went well at first and the Romans crossed the Tigris above Ctesiphon (see map VII, pages 210–11), then the capital of Persia. The Persians, unwilling to face so formidable an army, retired eastwards towards Hamadan (the ancient Ecbatana), destroying all supplies as they went. Lack of food obliged the Romans to retreat. On 26 June 363 Julian was wounded and died the same night. His had been the master-mind directing the whole operation and on his death the Roman army was glad to purchase its safe retreat by the surrender of Nisibis, Sinjar and five Roman provinces.

In 379, Theodosius began gradually to restore the unity and strength of the empire but he died in 395, bequeathing the eastern half of the empire to his elder son Arcadius, the western to his second son, Honorius. The empire was never again to be united. The western half was increasingly overrun by barbarians until, in 476, it finally ceased to exist. Thereafter Constantinople, the New Rome, became the capital of an empire consisting of the Balkans, Asia Minor, Syria, Palestine and Egypt.

Europeans are often pleased to think of the Roman Empire as an essentially Western power, based on Italy, France, Britain and Spain, but history does not support their claim. Before the rise of Rome, all the great civilizations of the world had originated from Asia. This pre-eminence, acquired during a period of several thousand years, could not easily be reversed. When, therefore, the empire broke in half, the Eastern or Byzantine Empire included most of the richest and the most civilized provinces.

From the military point of view, however, the Byzantine Empire was less happily situated. The whole Roman Empire, as we have seen, at the period of its greatest military power, had scarcely been a match for the aggressiveness of Persia. Now half that empire was left to continue the struggle alone.

The famous Emperor Justinian (527–65) devoted his long reign to the re-conquest of the West. In order to be free for this enterprise, however, he was obliged to buy peace from Persia in 532 by the payment of a large indemnity. In 534, however, the Persians invaded Syria and sacked Aleppo. Justinian once again was obliged to buy peace by the surrender of a number of cities.

In 540, the King of Persia was back again, advanced into the heart of Syria and sacked Edessa, Aleppo and Antioch itself, which was burned to the ground. After twenty years of war, during most of which the Persians had enjoyed the upper hand, peace was re-established on the old frontier.

In 602, the Persians were once more on the offensive. Chosroes Parviz invaded Syria and occupied Damascus. In 614, he captured Jerusalem, carrying away as a trophy the alleged 'True cross' of the Crucifixion. In 616, the Persians simultaneously conquered Egypt and Asia Minor and laid siege to Constantinople itself. The Eastern Roman Empire seemed to be about to disappear, as the Western had done in 476.

Not until 628 was peace restored on the basis of the frontiers of 602, after Syria and Palestine had suffered fourteen years of enemy occupation. Both empires were left in a state of ruin and bankruptcy.

Meanwhile, in 570, in a remote desert town of Arabia, a boy had been born, unknown alike to the mighty emperors and their great armies. His name was Muhammad and his work was destined to transform the history of Syria and indeed of the world.

Let us pause here for a moment to reconsider the history of Syria and Palestine prior to the reign of Islam. From the settlement of Pompey in 64 BC to the Arab conquest in AD 636, Syria had been Roman for seven hundred years. During the first thirty or forty years the corrupt rule of the republic had produced confusion and misery, but from the age of Augustus onwards, Syria and Palestine enjoyed no less than six hundred years of peace, wealth and prosperity.

To the modern citizen of Britain or the United States, six hundred years of peace seems utterly incredible. It is true that the peace of the empire as a whole was constantly disturbed both by the invasions of barbarians from the north and the endless civil wars between rival claimants to the purple. But such wars were fought out in Asia Minor, the Balkans, Italy or Gaul and rarely disturbed the peaceful progress of Syria.

Wars with Persia were a more serious threat but a careful comparison of their dates will show their rarity, when spaced over a period of six centuries. Moreover, when they did occur, the enemy normally captured Edessa, Aleppo or Antioch and then turned northwards into Asia Minor.

During these long centuries of progress, Syrian merchants invaded the whole Roman Empire, forming wealthy business communities as far afield as Paris, Spain and North Africa. After Rome itself, the greatest cities in the empire were Antioch in Syria and Alexandria in Egypt.

But even after six hundred years of Roman peace and prosperity, Syria retained her dual character. The sea coast from Antioch to Gaza and the province of Antioch itself were almost completely Graeco-Roman in culture, in religion and to a great extent also in race. But east of Lebanon and the Jordan, Semitic influences continued to predominate. The cities in culture, speech and appearance were Roman or Greek but the poor and the peasants continued to speak Aramaic, while the desert tribes migrating northwards from Arabia spoke Arabic.

This unceasing cross-fertilization by many advanced and varied cultures produced in Syria some of the most brilliant intellectuals in history and gave birth to the world's three greatest religions. Its influence can still be clearly traced in the quick-witted, emotional and brilliant intelligentsia of Syria and Palestine in our own times.

KEY DATES

4   From Muhammad to the coming of the Turks

WHEN THE PROPHET MUHAMMAD was born in Mecca, the peninsula of Arabia was principally inhabited by nomadic tribes. As we have seen, however, the East–West trade route, the wealthiest in the world, passed up the Red Sea or the Persian Gulf. Part of this commerce landed in the Yemen, or at the head of the Persian Gulf, and crossed the fringes of the Arabian deserts by camel-caravan.

While, therefore, the tribes of central Arabia were still primitive, there existed in certain areas civilized and sophisticated Arab communities which had, for several centuries, enjoyed familiar intercourse with the civilizations of Greece, Rome and Persia. In south Arabia, moreover, an Arab civilization had existed from a period many centuries before Christ. In the north we have seen the Nabataeans, an Arab commercial kingdom which included Damascus and, two centuries later, Palmyra, which dared dispute the empire of the East with Rome herself. A semi-Arab dynasty from Homs had provided four Roman emperors, while a fifth, Philip the Arabian, was probably a pure Arab from Bosra.

More advanced religions had also spread into Arabia. There were large Jewish settlements at Medina (then called Yathrib) and in the Yemen, where Christianity had also penetrated. Although most Arabs still worshipped idols, the influence of more spiritual religions was beginning to make itself felt. Mecca was a station on the caravan route from the Yemen to Egypt and Syria. The people of Mecca were merchants, and regularly travelled to Gaza and Damascus on business. A few of them had been touched by the desire for a more ethical and spiritual faith and one or two had adopted Christianity.

Muhammad is believed to have been born on 20 August 570. His father had died a few weeks before his birth. When he was six years old his mother died also. He was brought up at one time by a nurse, then by his grandfather, later by an uncle. Lonely and insecure, he grew up serious and pensive. At the age of twenty-five, he made at least one business trip to Damascus, during which tradition relates that he conversed with Christian monks. At twenty-five, Muhammad married a rich widow and was thus freed from the necessity of earning his living.

As he grew older, he became more and more devoted to solitude and meditation. At the age of forty, he saw a vision of the Archangel Gabriel and, three years later, he began to preach in Mecca. His message was simple. God, he alleged, was One, and idols must be swept away. One day the dead would rise again, the righteous to Paradise, the wicked to eternal punishment. He himself was the Messenger of God.

In support of this doctrine, he claimed Divine inspiration. At times, when a new message was coming to him, he would lie for a time covered with a blanket. When the revelation was over, he would dictate a new chapter of the Koran. His religion, which he called Islam – surrender to God – was based on its predecessors, Judaism and Christianity, both of which he recognized as divinely revealed, though both, he claimed, had fallen into heresy.

The town of Mecca contained a temple of idols, which brought considerable profit to the townspeople, who were indignant at Muhammad's demand for their abolition. After eight years of preaching, he had won only about seventy converts, while enduring much persecution. In 622, as a result, he escaped from Mecca to Medina, a town some two hundred miles to the north. Here he rapidly made converts and the movement began to spread to the surrounding tribes.

In Medina, the Prophet's attitude changed and he announced that God now commanded the Muslims to fight unbelievers. Eight years of desultory warfare ensued until, in January 630, the Prophet with

60

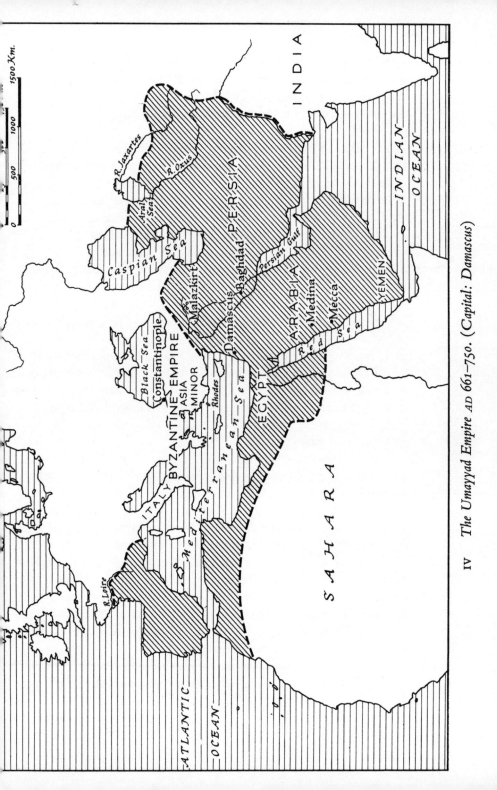

IV *The Umayyad Empire* AD 661–750. (*Capital: Damascus*)

ten thousand men captured the town of Mecca. Two years later, in June 632, Muhammad died in Medina. In the interval, nearly all the tribes of Arabia had submitted to his authority.

Abu Bekr, the Prophet's closest friend, assumed control as his khalifa (caliph) or successor. From time immemorial, the Arabian tribes had passed their time in fighting one another. The personal influence of the Prophet had temporarily restrained them but, once that influence was gone, it was doubtful how long internal peace could be maintained. Abu Bekr decided to employ the warlike energies of the tribes by invading Syria and Palestine.

In the Damascus area, a dynasty of Arab princes, Beni Ghassan, had for several generations been responsible, under the Byzantines, for defence against desert raids. The long wars against Persia had ruined the Byzantine economy and, in 628, the emperor abolished subsidies to the Arab tribes of Trans-Jordan, thereby weakening their loyalty. The Prophet had taught his followers that Muslims killed in war against non-Muslims would be instantly transported to Paradise, with the result that the early Muslims deliberately sought death in battle. The Byzantine army was well trained and equipped, but nothing could resist these torrents of wild tribesmen, intent on finding death and Paradise.

The Arab conquest of Syria and Palestine took a little more than two years. The final decisive battle was fought on 20 August 636, on the River Yarmouk, near the site of the modern town of Deraa, on the road from Damascus to Amman. (See map VII, pages 210–11.) The Byzantines retired through the Taurus Mountains to Asia Minor and all Syria and Palestine passed under Muslim rule.

Muhammad's first three successors or caliphs had retained Medina as the capital. Meanwhile, however, the Arabs had conquered Egypt, North Africa and Persia, and had become a great empire. The little, out-of-the-way, desert town of Medina was no longer an adequate capital and, in 661, the seat of the imperial government was moved to Damascus.

For some thirty years after the Prophet's death, the Arab Empire remained a theocracy, in which religion was almost the sole preoccupation. Muawiya, the first caliph to rule from Damascus, transformed this Muslim theocracy into an Arab secular empire. Soon their victorious armies had reached the Atlantic in what we call Morocco. Although desert dwellers, they had built fleets, seized Cyprus and Rhodes and raided Sicily. In the east, they had conquered all Persia, and what we call Afghanistan and Soviet Uzbekistan. Syria found itself the mother country of the world's greatest empire.

As conquerors, the Arabs behaved with exemplary self-control. The conquered peoples were offered three courses. Firstly, if they became Muslims, they were recognized, in theory at least, as the equals of the conquerors. Secondly, those who remained Christians were obliged to pay a poll tax and their social position was inferior to Muslims, but their persons and property were safe. The third course open to them was to fight on.

The inhabitants of Syria and Palestine were Christians. Those living in the Mediterranean coastal plain had completely adopted Roman and Greek culture. In eastern Syria and Trans-Jordan, the people were largely of Semitic or Arab stock, but they also were Christians. The nomadic Arab tribes of the Syrian desert were rapidly converted to Islam. The villagers of eastern Syria were more tenacious of their Christianity. The population of the coastal plains, particularly from Lebanon to Antioch, were unwilling to adopt Islam and many have retained their Christian religion down to our own times.

The admiration felt in Europe for the ancient Romans has largely distorted our view of history. The successors of Rome, whether Byzantine Christians or Muslim Arabs, have received scant justice from European historians. One of the most remarkable features of the people of central Arabia was their adaptability. Arriving in the highly sophisticated society of Byzantine Syria, they quickly adapted themselves to their new surroundings. Within fifty or sixty years, they had completely taken over and arabicized the competent Byzantine administrative machinery and were studying the art, literature, history and theology of their predecessors. The Dome of the Rock in Jerusalem, for example, one of the most beautiful and unique buildings in the world, was erected in the reign of the Caliph Abdul Malik ibn Merwan (685–705).

One of the most remarkable features of the Arab conquests was their small numbers. In AD 700, for example, there were only 45,000 Arab Muslims in the province of Damascus, and only twenty thousand in that of Homs. The great majority of the people of Syria and Palestine, numbering probably some five millions, were still of mixed Aramaean-Greek-Hittite descent and were Christians.

Many of the conquering Arab tribes went on to fight in North Africa or in Persia. Others preferred to remain as nomads in the desert like their ancestors. The remainder moved into the great cities, where they became a ruling aristocracy. The cultivators and villagers were at first untouched and their way of life was scarcely changed by the Arab conquest.

The Prophet had authorized the use of women captured in war as concubines. The amazing extent of the Arab conquests had enabled them to acquire great numbers of such foreign concubines, Greeks, Persians, Armenians, Egyptians and North African Berbers. All the offspring of an Arab father were accepted as Arabs. Thus a few generations after the conquest, the 'Arabs' of Syria were ethnologically a different race from the conquerors who had emerged from Arabia after the death of the Prophet.

Syria had been the capital of the Seleucid Empire for two hundred years. Under the Arabs, she became once more an imperial capital, but of an empire vastly greater than that of Seleucus. In the reign of the Caliph Waleed (705–15), the Arab Empire attained an extent half as big again as that of Rome in its heyday. In the West, it included Spain, southern France and all North Africa. In the East, it embraced modern Iraq, Persia, West Pakistan and Soviet Turkestan to the borders of China, north of Tibet.

All the Umayyads beautified Damascus, their capital, but Waleed probably more than any other. The palace of the caliphs was completely paved with green marble, the ceilings glistened with gold, the walls with fine mosaics. In the main court-yard was a great basin of water, fed by ever-flowing fountains and cascades which diffused a fragrant coolness. These irrigated a garden, planted

64

with the most beautiful trees and plants and animated by the songs of countless exotic singing birds. In the inner apartments reclined the most beautiful women to be found anywhere in the world.

Meanwhile, however, social and political pressures were at work. The Prophet had declared all Muslims to be equal, regardless of race. The conquests had, on the other hand, been accomplished by Arabs, who had thereby become a ruling class and treated non-Arab Muslims with condescension. The latter became increasingly discontented and pressed their claim to that equality to which the Prophet had said that all Muslims were entitled.

All the caliphs who had ruled since the Prophet's death had been members of his family, which was known as Quraish. Rivalry, however, had already appeared between different branches, Muhammad himself having left no son. The Damascus caliphs, known as the Umayyads, had been descended from a cousin of his called Umayya. Now another branch claimed the caliphate, the descendants of the Prophet's uncle, Abbas.

Syria, seat of the empire, was loyal to the Umayyads but the Abbasids were supported by the Persian Muslims, who resented Arab domination. In 747, rebellion broke out in east Persia, and in June 750, Damascus was captured and the Umayyad dynasty came to an end after reigning in Damascus for ninety years. The Prophet had been dead for 118 years.

The Abbasids had been largely raised to power by the support of the non-Arab Muslims of the east, principally the Persians. With Syria still secretly loyal to the Umayyads, the new dynasty found it advisable to move their capital to the banks of the Tigris. Mansur, the second Abbasid caliph, founded the city of Baghdad whence he could at need call on his Persian supporters for help. The move was to change world history down to our own times.

Syria, Palestine, North Africa and the Mediterranean basin had for nearly a thousand years been subject to Greek and Roman sovereignty and culture. For the same period, the Euphrates-Tigris valley which we now call Iraq had been part of Persia. The transference of the capital from Damascus to Baghdad resulted in the gradual orientalization of the Muslim Empire.

The new caliphs were, of course, Arabs from Mecca and the background of the empire continued to be Arab, but the high offices of state were no longer the sole prerogative of Arabs. Persians began to occupy important positions and Persian troops were increasingly enlisted in the imperial armies. Under the Abbasids of Baghdad, Damascus ceased to be the imperial capital but Syria continued to enjoy peace and prosperity.

The Arabs reached the height of their glory in the reign of Harun al Rashid (786–809). Harun invaded Asia Minor nine times and lesser raids against the Byzantines took place almost every summer. Baghdad being too far from the frontier to enable the caliph to superintend these operations, he built himself a palace at Raqqa in Syria on the Euphrates. (See map III, page 43.)

In the ninth century, Arab ships were sailing regularly to China, Malacca, Java, and Sumatra, as well as Ceylon and India. On the east coast of Africa, Arab merchants did business at least as far south as Madagascar. One of the most extraordinary features of the Arab Empire was the profusion of gold. Not only did the caliphs use it for coinage but it was plastered on the buckles of their belts, their weapons and their saddles and bridles. Meanwhile in Europe, Charlemagne, a contemporary of Harun, was unable to maintain a gold currency, the precious metal being unobtainable in Europe.

The reign of Harun's son, Mamun (813–33), was scarcely less brilliant than that of his father. Under Harun, the high noon of commercial wealth had been achieved. Under Mamun, the Arabs reached the stage of intellectualism. If the transfer of the capital from Damascus to Baghdad weakened Arab imperial power in the Mediterranean, it gave a decided impetus to intellectual activity. In the West, the leading kings and nobles were unable to read and write, but Baghdad was centrally placed between the Greek culture of Constantinople and the ancient civilizations of Persia, India and China.

At the Baghdad academy or House of Wisdom, the works of Aristotle and Plato and the medical textbooks of Galen and Hippocrates were diligently translated into Arabic. The work of translation was carried out under the caliph's personal supervision in the House of Wisdom but the translators from the Greek were mostly Syrian Christians, whose proximity to the Byzantine frontier made them bilingual in Arabic and Greek. The best known of them was Hunain ibn Ishaq, himself a famous physician in his own right.

From India came the decimal system and the numerals which we still use and call 'Arabic'. Astronomy had always been a favourite science since Chaldaean times and was now immensely enriched by the simultaneous study of Greek and Indian astronomy. The principal Persian contribution lay in the fields of literature and art, while the manufacture of paper – to diffuse this knowledge – was learned from the Chinese. The reign of Mamun constituted one of the most extraordinary outbursts of intellectual activity in history.

In the last four years of his reign, Mamun led four successive invasions of Byzantine territory. The advanced base for these operations was Tarsus, the birthplace of St Paul, which was then in Syria but is now in Turkey. (See map III, page 43.)

A significant event of the reign of Mamun was the grant of autonomy to east Persia, as a result of which Persian troops became increasingly unreliable. To replace them, the caliph bought Turkish slave boys known as Mamelukes from east of the Aral Sea, an area now known as Soviet Turkistan. These youths made splendid soldiers until they began to realize that they held the military power and that the caliph was in reality at their mercy. Finally, on 10 December 861, the Turkish mercenaries assassinated the Caliph Mutawakkil and set up a military dictatorship in Baghdad.

For 230 years, the caliphs, in Damascus or in Baghdad, had enjoyed an extraordinary degree of power and splendour. They were not only despotic rulers but, as members of the Prophet's family, enjoyed an aura of religious sanctity. As soon as the provinces realized that the caliphs had become the helpless puppets of their own Turkish mercenaries, the empire fell to pieces.

For some two centuries and a half the Arabs had dominated the then-known world, with the exception of China. In the early part of the eighth century, they held Spain and half of France. Later they lost most of France but occupied Sicily and southern Italy. The transfer of the capital of the empire from Syria to Iraq, however, had gradually weakened their imperial control of the Mediterranean.

From 861 onwards, after the murder of the Caliph Mutawakkil, the Arabs lost their military power, partly owing to the gradual alienation of the tribes from the government, for it was the tribesmen who had provided the best soldiers. The cultural leadership was, however, to survive for another 250 years, in spite of the fact that they had lost political power to the still barbarian Turks, most of whom were illiterate.

The age of translation from Greek, Sanscrit and Persian sources had lasted for a century (750–850) culminating in the reign of Mamun. Thereafter the Arabs themselves became pioneers of science, philosophy and literature. The earliest known treatise on opthalmology was published by Hunain ibn Ishaq in about 860. ·

The earliest known chemist's shops were established at this time in Baghdad, the pharmacists being obliged to pass a public examination before starting business. In 931, physicians were forbidden to practise until they had passed an examination and been granted a diploma. In that year, there were said to be 860 qualified physicians in Baghdad. Government doctors made daily visits to the prisons to examine the prisoners.

The first public hospital was opened in the reign of Harun al Rashid. Within a few years, every large city had its hospital, complete with its dispensary, library of medical works and courses of training for medical students. Two physicians of international repute wrote in Arabic at this period, Al Razi (850–923) and Ibn Sina, known in Europe as Avicenna. Among innumerable other works, Al Razi's *Treatise on smallpox and measles* contains the earliest known clinical account of smallpox. It is true that many of these intellectual activities took place in Baghdad but a considerable number of the intellectuals were Syrians, who had gone to work in the imperial capital as, in an earlier age, they had migrated to Rome.

Al Mamun's astronomers measured the circumference of the earth with remarkable accuracy, six hundred years before Europe admitted it to be round. Some of the experiments leading to this result were carried out on the flat plains south of Palmyra.

68

The Turkish military dictators, who maintained the Abbasid caliphs as figureheads, were able to exercise a precarious control over Iraq, but their authority rarely extended to Egypt or Syria. From 861 to 972, a succession of Turkish army officers seized power in Egypt and endeavoured to annex Syria also. The situation, however, remained unstable, even verging upon anarchy.

We have already seen that the Arab Empire had been more than once disturbed by rivalries between the Umayyads and the Abbasids, different branches of the Prophet's family. In 972, a major change took place in the situation, when an alleged descendant of Ali, Muhammad's cousin and son-in-law, seized power in Egypt and established a dynasty. They called themselves the Fatimids, after Fatima, the Prophet's daughter and the wife of Ali, from whom they claimed descent. After founding Cairo as their capital, they sent their armies to occupy Syria and Palestine also.

The following table illustrates the three dynasties of caliphs, the Umayyads, the Fatimids and the Abbasids. The supporters of the Fatimids were called Shiites.

GENEALOGY OF THE ARAB CALIPHS

ABID MENAF

ABID SHAMS   HASHIM

UMAYYA   ABDUL MUTTALIB

Umayyad caliphs   ABU TALIB   ABDULLA   ABBAS
of Damascus,
and later of   MUHAMMAD THE PROPHET
Spain

            ALI ══════ FATIMA   Abbasid caliphs
                       (no sons)   of Baghdad

        Fatimid caliphs of Egypt

This development was disastrous for Syria. From 661 to 972, Egypt had been no more than a province under the caliphs of Damascus or Baghdad. Now the Fatimids of Egypt assumed the title of caliph in direct challenge to the Abbasids of Baghdad. Syria found herself once more the 'causeway' lying between the rival powers in Cairo and Baghdad.

In fact, however, Syria did not become the cockpit between the Fatimids and the Abbasids. For three centuries, the Byzantine Empire had suffered terrible disasters at the hands of the Arabs. Now the chaotic situation in the Arab countries presented the Byzantines with the opportunity for revenge. In the thirty-eight years from 962 to 1000, Syria suffered no less than eight major invasions, led by successive Byzantine emperors. One of these incursions reached as far south as Tiberias on the Sea of Galilee. The Byzantines had not enough troops to enable them to annex and garrison Syria. The countryside was ravaged without pity, the crops and the villages were burned, the vineyards and orchards reduced to deserts and the young men and girls were driven away to slavery. Neither the Abbasid caliph in Baghdad nor the Fatimid in Cairo raised a finger to defend Syria. The only serious opposition was offered by Ibn Hamdan, an Arab prince of Aleppo, who was not afraid frequently to engage the Byzantine emperor himself in battle. Ultimately the Byzantines annexed Antioch and moved their frontier east of the Taurus Mountains to the Euphrates.

In 996, the Fatimid Caliph Hakim had come to the throne of Egypt. Anarchy in Iraq had diverted the oriental trade from the Persian Gulf to the Red Sea and Egypt was wealthy and prosperous. Syria, however, was in constant rebellion against Egyptian attempts to annex her. A contemporary Arab writer remarked that, of all the Islamic nations, none was more submissive to their rulers than the Egyptians and none more rebellious than those of Damascus. All the features of this situation are exactly repeated today.

In 1018, the Caliph Hakim became insane and declared himself to be God. On 13 February 1021 he was assassinated in Cairo. A man by the name of Ismail al Darazi, who had been a fervid partisan of the mad caliph, fled from Egypt and took refuge in the mountains of Lebanon, where he preached the divinity of his master. He founded a closely-knit religious community who, after his name, were called Druzes and who still play a prominent part in Syria and Lebanon. The details of their religion are secret and are known only to their own elders. Those aspiring to be elders are obliged to undergo a series of initiations before they are admitted to full knowledge of their own faith.

The Druzes, having survived for 950 years as a persecuted sect, have a high reputation as fighters. For the same reason, when alone in the midst of another community, they are said to be allowed to pretend adherence to another faith. Sometimes, when asked about their religion, they will claim to be Muslims.

Since the murder of the Caliph Mutawakkil in 861, Iraq and Persia had been divided up between rival military dictators, most of them Turks. These men were the descendants of the soldier slaves introduced by the caliphs, who had entered the empire as individuals and had become Muslims. In the first half of the eleventh century, however, a new scourge appeared. A complete tribe of wild Turkish nomads, known as the Ghuzz, burst into northern Persia from the central Asian steppes. Under their chiefs, known as the Seljuqs, they swept across northern Persia to Armenia, massacring, looting and raping as they went.

In the year 1050, Tughril Beg, the first Seljuq sultan, captured Baghdad, reducing the Abbasid caliph to the status of a vassal and depriving him of all political power. In 1071, Alp Arslan, the successor of Tughril Beg, completely defeated the Byzantine emperor at Malazkirt, twenty miles north of Lake Van. The Byzantine army was virtually annihilated. By 1080, the Seljuqs had conquered all Asia Minor and reached the shores of the Bosphorus opposite Constantinople.

In 1071, the year of Malazkirt, the Seljuqs also occupied Syria and Palestine, driving the Fatimids back to Egypt. Eight years later, in 1079, the brother of Sultan Alp Arslan established himself in Damascus as King of Syria.

For four centuries Europe had lived in fear of the imperialism of the Arabs who had, at various times, conquered Spain, southern France, Sicily, southern Italy and Crete. Throughout this period, however, Europe's eastern flank had been firmly held by the Byzantine Empire. Now, with that empire on the verge of collapse, it seemed as if the Muslims might come pouring into the Balkans and invade Europe from the East.

Asia Minor, the best Byzantine recruiting ground, had been lost, and the Emperor Alexius Comnenus found himself short of men. In 1095, he sent an embassy to the Pope, seeking his support for the recruitment of mercenaries in Europe. On 27 November 1095, at Clermont in France, the Pope issued an appeal for men to march to the relief of their fellow Christians in the East. The Crusades had begun.

KEY DATES

1 (*right*) Baalism, the worship of many local gods, was the religion of the Canaanites, some of the earliest inhabitants of the Syro-Palestine area. This stele of the Canaanite Baal, Hadad, was found at Ras Shamra and dates from the first half of the second millennium BC.

2 (*far right*) Dating from the same period is this bronze seated goddess.

3 By the eighth century BC Phoenicians, who then lived on the coastal plain, came into conflict with the Assyrians. This repoussé bronze band shows, at the top, tribute being carried by Phoenicians to the Assyrians who are illustrated on the lower band as a marching army.

4   This relief shows the Commisariat of the Assyrian army at the siege and capture
of Lachish by Sennacherib in 701 BC.

5   Darius I the Great was the king of the Persian empire which by the fifth
century BC included Syro-Palestine. This contemporary relief shows Darius (seated
on throne) with Xerxes, his son, standing behind him.

6   The Persian empire fell in 333 BC when Darius III was defeated by Alexander the Great at Issus. Paolo Veronese's (c. 1528–88) beautiful painting of Darius' family submitting to Alexander reflects a somewhat fanciful interpretation.

7   A marked contrast and doubtless nearer the visual truth is this fragment of a mosaic from Pompeii showing Alexander making his final attack on Darius III.

8 (*right*) In 64 BC Syria became a Roman province and by *c.* 29 BC Augustus had made Baalbek (in the modern Lebanon) a Roman colony. The famous remains of the Temple of Jupiter dominate the landscape.

9 (*below left*) Septimius Severus, a Roman army officer, was made Emperor in AD 193. This contemporary painting shows him with his Syrian wife Julia Domna and his son Caracalla.

10 (*below right*) This beautiful fragment of a Roman mosaic pavement at Bait Mery reflects the magnificent skill of the Romans.

(*left*) At Byblos in Lebanon, the modern Jubail,
s Roman amphitheatre provided entertainment.

(*below left*) The city of Jerash in Jordan, once
e of the cities of the Decapolis, reflects much of
e grandeur of Graeco-Roman city planning. This
autifully preserved oval colonnaded forum dates
m the third century A D.

(*right*) Petra in Jordan was once the capital of the
abataean Kingdom (*c*. 300 B C–A D 105). The
agnificent tombs with their classical Roman façades
e cut into the face of the cliff.

(*below*) Palmyra in Syria, an oasis surrounded
deserts, was already a meeting-place for caravans in
oo B C. In A D 130 it was visited by Hadrian who
creased its fortifications against the Parthians. In
e foreground is the triumphal archway. The castle
the background is Arab.

15 This view of Tyre from the air illustrates its strength as a fortress and its commercial harbour for sea-faring trade.

16 Aleppo was long a centre for the caravan trade from Persia and the East. The town, here seen from the air, is dominated by the citadel.

5 The Crusades

In Roman days, western Europe had been a wealthy, commercial community based on the cities. But when, in the seventh
century, the Arab Empire extended from Morocco to China and
held naval command of the Mediterranean, Europe, for four centuries, was cut off from world trade and became an agricultural
continent. In the absence of money, land became wealth and the
cities fell into ruin. The leaders of the people were no longer bankers
and businessmen but landowners and barons. When Pope Urban
II preached his crusade in 1095, therefore, there were no regular
armies in Europe, for no one had the cash to pay them.

Four independent 'divisions' set out in response to the Pope's call,
each commanded by a great lord and consisting of his tenants and
feudatories. Godfrey de Bouillon, Duke of Lower Lotharingia
(approximately modern Belgium) and of Lorraine, commanded the
first. Robert, Duke of Normandy, eldest son of William the Conqueror, was leader of the second. The third had been raised by
Raymond de Saint Gilles, Count of Toulouse, and the commander of the fourth was Bohemond, Count of Apulia, of the
Norman Hauteville family which had conquered southern Italy.

The Crusaders were ferried across the Bosphorus early in 1097
and set out to attack the Turks in Asia Minor. In order to protect
Europe from invasion from the east, the obvious requirement was to
drive the Seljuqs from Asia Minor, restore the Byzantine Empire as
it had been before the Battle of Malazkirt and then, if necessary, leave
sufficient military forces to enable the Byzantines to hold their own.

This simple military requirement, however, became confused in
the minds of the western Crusaders with the emotional objective of

81

recovering Jerusalem. Sweeping across Asia Minor, they invaded northern Syria and, in October 1097, laid siege to Antioch. Meanwhile the Seljuq Turks closed in again on Asia Minor, cutting the land communications between the Crusaders and Europe.

On 3 June 1098 the Crusaders captured Antioch, but not until 13 January 1099, did they start southwards for Jerusalem. Following the valley of the Orontes to begin with, they turned through the gap in the mountains west of Homs, emerging on the coast near Tripoli, which, however, they failed to take, ultimately reaching Jerusalem unopposed on 7 June. After heavy fighting, the Holy City was carried by assault on 15 July 1099.

The Crusaders now found themselves in the same predicament as Syria had been so often before – in a central position with enemies in Asia Minor, Iraq and Egypt. Their situation was extremely precarious because, far from holding all Syria and Palestine, they were in actual occupation of only two cities, Antioch and Jerusalem.

No sooner had the Crusaders taken Jerusalem than the arrival at Asqalon of a relieving army from Egypt was reported to them. At dawn on 12 August 1099 the Egyptian army was surprised and utterly defeated outside Asqalon. Godfrey de Bouillon was elected King of Jerusalem but refused the royal title, preferring the modest appellation of Defender of the Holy Sepulchre. 'He would not', he said, 'wear a crown of gold where his Master had worn a crown of thorns.'

After the capture of Jerusalem, the vast majority of the Crusaders returned to Europe, Godfrey being left with only three hundred mounted men and two thousand foot. Raymond de Saint Gilles marched away to the north and carved out an independent state for himself, assuming the title of Count of Tripoli. Further north, Bohemond had proclaimed himself Prince of Antioch while Baldwin, Godfrey's brother, had moved inland and made himself Count of Edessa.

Thus the Crusaders had established four autonomous states, the Kingdom of Jerusalem, the County of Tripoli, the Princedom of Antioch and the County of Edessa. Apart from the County of Edessa, the population of which was largely Armenian, the

V   *Syria during the Crusades*

Crusaders held the coastal plains west of the Jordan and the mountains of Lebanon, the same areas as had previously been Hellenized for a thousand years and which we have seen had thoughout history been largely non-Semitic.

Syria proper and Trans-Jordan, the essentially Semitic areas, with the great cities of Aleppo, Hama, Homs and Damascus remained in Muslim hands. Thus the Crusaders split Syria and Palestine along the north and south line which had always divided the Semitic from the partly non-Semitic areas.

The Crusaders, with their small numbers of men, were able to hold on because the Seljuq Empire had fallen into anarchy. The great Sultan Malik Shah had died in 1092, five years before the arrival of the First Crusade, and civil war had immediately broken out in Persia between his four sons. The Seljuqs had meanwhile replaced the native Arab princes of Syria by Turkish warlords who held the country on a feudal basis. So jealous were these Turkish lords of one another that cooperation between them against the Crusaders was impossible.

In our rather cynical times, it has become fashionable to say that the Crusades were not a religious movement at all but were inspired by economic motives. The facts of the First Crusade disprove the charge. To begin with, the origin of the Crusades was an appeal for help from the Byzantine emperor, half of whose territory had been overrun by the Seljuqs and whose capital was threatened. The origin of the First Crusade was, therefore, not offensive but defensive.

It is true that the Crusaders soon lost sight of this plain military objective in favour of the emotional appeal of rescuing the Holy Sepulchre for Christendom, but the emphasis placed on the conquest of Jerusalem itself proves that the motive was religious. We may today consider that Christianity should not be defended by force of arms and that the Crusaders were wrong in trying to do so, but this does not alter the fact that their motive was religious, even if mistaken.

The charge that the leaders of the First Crusade were greedy barons anxious to acquire estates in Asia is the usual basis of the accusation of economic objectives. The fact, however, that once Jerusalem was taken, the majority of the Crusaders returned home, leaving Godfrey with only two hundred knights to defend the Holy City, proves that most of the Crusaders had no ambitions in the East. They had vowed to re-conquer Jerusalem and once their vow was accomplished, they left for home.

Finally, the fact that Godfrey, Raymond, Bohemond and Baldwin did become rulers of autonomous states is held to prove that this had been their objective all along and that it was dictated by greed. Incidentally all four of these were great nobles in Europe and were certainly not poor and landless. The point frequently overlooked, however, is that the feudal system was the only form of government which these men knew. The basis of this system was that armies were maintained not, as we do, by paying the troops in cash, but by giving them land.

It is obvious that it would have been useless to conquer Jerusalem if no army had been left to defend it, but the only way these men knew of maintaining an army was by giving the soldiers land. There was, therefore, no other method by which the Crusaders could continue to defend Jerusalem other than by seizing land and settling their soldiers upon it.

It is true that the Crusaders were rough, ignorant, simple semi-barbarians, far behind the Syrians in culture and civilization. This, however, does not destroy the fact that, according to their lights, their motives were religious. When the Crusades ended two hundred years later, the spirit of the First Crusade had long ago evaporated. The Crusaders who had settled down in the East had become civilized as a result of their contact with the Arabs and were largely pre-occupied with commerce. Two centuries, however, is a long time and the last Crusaders lived in a world which had completely lost the spirit of the first.

Godfrey died in 1100 and was succeeded, first by his brother, Baldwin I and then by his cousin, Baldwin II. The latter died in 1131 leaving three daughters. Count Fulk of Anjou[4] married the eldest and reigned as King of Jerusalem until he was killed in 1143, leaving a twelve-year-old son, Baldwin III.

From 1099 to 1144, desultory fighting had never ceased between the Crusaders and the Muslims but Godfrey, the two Baldwins and Fulk had all been strong kinds and the Turkish warlords had failed to cooperate. In 1127, however, Zengi, a former slave of the Seljuqs, seized Nisibin, Harran and Aleppo. (See map VII, pages 210–11, Nisibis under the Romans was called Nisibin by the Arabs.) The Seljuqs of Persia had vanished but in Zengi a new and dominating personality confronted the Crusaders. In December 1144, Zengi captured Edessa by surprise and one of the four Crusader states ceased to exist.

In 1146, Zengi was murdered but was succeeded by his even more redoubtable son, Nur al Din. The fall of Edessa provoked the Second Crusade, led by the Emperor of Germany and the King of France. The Crusaders were defeated outside Damascus and the whole expedition ended in fiasco. In 1154, Nur al Din seized Damascus from its Turkish lord and thereby united all Syria and the Jezira.

In Egypt, the Fatimid caliphs were completely decadent. The Crusaders and Nur al Din were evenly balanced. If either side could seize the wealth of Egypt, it would become predominant. Both armies invaded the Nile delta. In 1169, however, Nur al Din sent a force of overwhelming strength and the Crusaders were obliged to evacuate Egypt.

The Syrian army had been commanded by Shirkuh, a Kurdish soldier of fortune, who was accompanied by his nephew Salah al Din, better known to us as Saladin. Two months later, Shirkuh died and Saladin became viceroy of Egypt for Nur al Din. In 1174, Nur al Din himself died, leaving a young boy as his heir. Saladin immediately marched on Syria, defeated the family of his late master, Nur al Din, and made himself sultan of an empire extending from Mosul on the Tigris to the western desert of Egypt.

The Muslims were now immensely stronger than the Crusaders, both in manpower and resources, and were commanded by the capable Saladin. By contrast, the King of Jerusalem, Baldwin IV, was a boy who was dying of leprosy, and the Crusader states were in anarchy.

On 4 July 1187 the Crusaders were utterly defeated at Hattin and on 2 October 1187 Saladin took Jerusalem. Within the next two years, he had occupied all the Crusader states except for Tyre, Tripoli and a small area dependent on Antioch.

The fall of Jerusalem roused public opinion in the West and the Third Crusade set out under Philip Augustus, King of France, and Richard Cœur de Lion, King of England. Acre was besieged and taken on 11 July 1191. Philip Augustus then returned to France and Richard became sole commander. From Acre he marched down the coast to Jaffa, defeating Saladin on the way at Arsoof.

Richard fortified Jaffa as a base for the advance on Jerusalem but the latter city was built on a rocky range of mountains 2500 feet high. The Crusader army was militarily too weak to climb the mountains in the face of Saladin's superior numbers. As a result a stalemate ensued. The Muslims were exhausted and Richard was anxious to return home. On 3 September 1192 peace was signed. The Crusader states were reconstituted on the coastal plain from Jaffa to Antioch, but Jerusalem was not recovered.

Chivalrous relations were maintained between Richard and Saladin, who exchanged correspondence throughout the war. Richard's prowess was almost incredible. In a battle outside Jaffa, he fought the Muslim army almost single-handed. 'The King of England', wrote an Arab historian, 'rode up and down the whole length of our army, without any of our men venturing to attack him.' After the battle, Saladin sent Richard a gift of fruit and iced drinks, cooled with snow from Mount Hermon.

Saladin was succeeded by his brother and then by his nephew, both of whom proved to be just and capable rulers over an empire which extended from Mosul on the Tigris to the western desert of Egypt. The chivalrous relations established between Saladin and Richard were maintained between his descendants, the Ayoubid dynasty, and the leaders of the Crusader states, many of whom were now the fourth or the fifth generation born in Syria or Palestine. They had many Muslim friends and had become half Syrian in their mentality.

The Crusading spirit, however, was not yet extinguished in the West and successive Popes continued to preach new crusades.

Richard's inability to climb the mountainous range on which Jerusalem is built made the Crusaders adopt a plan to invade Egypt. In May 1218, the Fifth Crusade landed in the mouth of the Nile and laid siege to Damietta. It was commanded by Jean de Brienne, who had become King of Jerusalem by marrying the heiress to the throne, there being no surviving male heirs. The campaign ended in disaster, the Muslims cutting the banks of the Nile in flood and sub-merging the Crusader army.

The most ironical of all the Crusades was the Sixth. The Sultan al Kamil, the nephew of Saladin, faced with a revolt in Syria, invited Frederick II, Emperor of Germany, to come to Palestine and help him. Frederick was engaged in a struggle for power with the Pope, who had excommunicated him. Hoping to strengthen his hand against the Pope by retaking Jerusalem, the emperor landed at Acre on 7 September 1228. On this remarkable Crusade, the leader had been excommunicated by the Pope but had been invited to come by the sultan.

No fighting took place but Frederick obtained a number of con-cessions by negotiation. The Christians were allowed to re-occupy the greater party of the city of Jerusalem, on condition that they did not fortify it. A few years later, however, after the death of Sultan Kamil, it was re-occupied by the Muslims.

On 5 June 1249 the Seventh Crusade, commanded by Saint Louis IX, King of France, landed at Damietta. He hoped to succeed where Jean de Brienne had failed but the expedition likewise ended in disaster.

From Saladin's assumption of command in Egypt in 1171 until its collapse in 1250, the Ayoubid dynasty lasted seventy-nine years. Throughout most of this period, Muslims and Crusaders maintained the chivalrous relations established by Saladin and Richard Cœur de Lion.

The Crusaders living in the Holy Land, however, were now very different from the stern warriors of Godfrey de Bouillon and the First Crusade. A hundred and fifty years of residence on the sunny shores of the eastern Mediterranean had damped their religious ardour but sharpened their wits. The rugged military virtues of their forbears had given place to a propensity for political intrigue and commercial profits. They were educated and cultured and had acquired an Arab standard of living, still much more luxurious than that of western Europe.

Every petty baron defended his own interests, while large business communities of Venetians, Genoese and Pisans competed bitterly with each other for commercial profits. A considerable part of the oriental trade, which for thousands of years had enriched Syria and Egypt, passed through the Crusader ports of Acre, Tripoli and Antioch, from which it was carried in Italian ships to Europe.

It will be remembered that the Abbasid caliphs in the ninth century had started the practice of recruiting their armies from Turkish slave boys, and that these Mamelukes had murdered the caliph and wrecked the Arab Empire. Saladin's family, the Ayoubids, repeated the same error. The army with which Saladin fought Richard Cœur de Lion had consisted largely of Turkish Mamelukes, assisted by Kurdish and Arab tribesmen.

On 1 May 1250 the last Ayoubid sultan, Turan Shah, a great-nephew of Saladin, was murdered in Egypt by the Mamelukes of his own army. The Ayoubid Empire thereupon broke up. In Damascus, a great-grandson of Saladin, Malik al Nasir Yusuf, proclaimed himself King of Syria. The Mamelukes seized control of Egypt.

KEY DATES

1095	Pope Urban II preaches the First Crusade in answer to appeal from the Byzantine Emperor
1099	Crusader capture of Jerusalem
1187	Recapture of Jerusalem by Saladin
1189–92	Re-establishment of the Crusader states by Richard Cœur de Lion but without Jerusalem
1250	Murder of Sultan Turan Shah and collapse of the Ayoubid Empire

6   Mamelukes and Mongols: 1250–1517

IN THE FIRST HALF OF THE THIRTEENTH CENTURY a new and terrible scourge afflicted the Muslim world. In central Asia, a group of tribes known to us as the Mongols roamed the plains and mountains south of Lake Baikal, east of the Turkic tribes who had already more than once invaded Persia, Iraq and Syria.

In 1211–15, the Mongols under Jenghis Khan conquered northern China and Korea. In 1220, Jenghis Khan laid waste the greater part of Persia and what is now south Russia. In 1227, however, Jenghis Khan died and Syria seemed to have escaped the storm.

Wherever the Mongols went, they used the same technique. Marching across the country, they swept up all the young men and carried them with them as slaves. The other inhabitants were killed. On reaching a walled city, the slave prisoners were set to work to surround it completely with a ditch and breastwork, a task normally completed in twenty-four hours. The walls were then bombarded until a breach was made, whereupon the prisoners were driven up the breach in front of the assaulting troops. When the city was taken, all the inhabitants were killed, regardless of age or sex, and the city was burned and razed to the ground.

In 1258, Hulagu, a grandson of Jenghis Khan, took and utterly destroyed Baghdad. The last Abbasid caliph, Mustasim, was killed and the caliphate virtually came to an end. Hulagu then spent the winter in Tabriz, south of the Caucasus. In January 1260, he appeared before Aleppo. Malik al Nasir Yusuf, the great-grandson of Saladin, whom we left in the last chapter as King of Syria, fled to

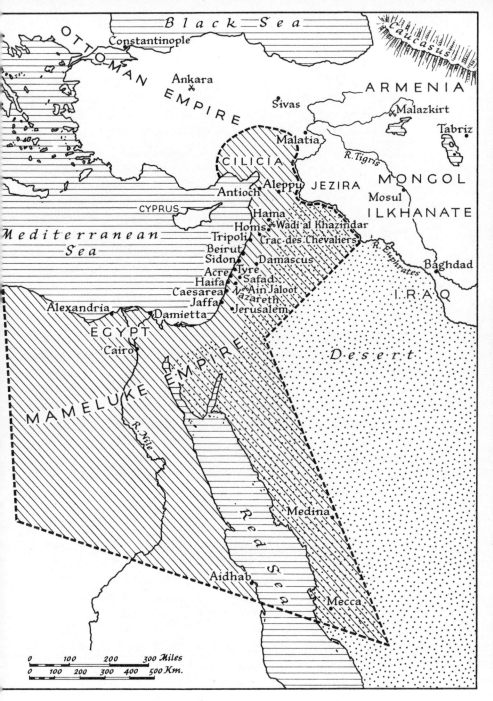

VI   *The Mameluke Empire at its greatest extent*

Egypt without fighting a battle. On 20 January 1260 Aleppo was carried by storm, the city destroyed and the inhabitants massacred. Hulagu announced his intention of taking Damascus and then of conquering Egypt – threats which he might easily have carried out, for no one dared to oppose the Mongols in the field.

When the Mongols had been a group of nomad tribes, it had been their custom on the death of the Great Khan to gather at a point on the steppes to elect a successor. Although their armies were now deployed from China to Hungary and Syria, they still adhered to this custom. Damascus was saved from destruction by the death in Mongolia of the Great Khan Mangu. Hulagu marched away in haste for Mongolia, leaving only some 25,000 men in Syria under a commander called Kitbugha, a Nestorian Christian. The surrender of Damascus was accepted and the city was occupied by Kitbugha without a massacre on 1 March 1260.

It will be remembered that, after the murder of the last Ayoubid sultan, the Mamelukes of that dynasty had set up their own govern/ ment in Cairo. Their system consisted of a military dictatorship. The army was composed of Turkish ex/slave boys, most of whom could not even speak Arabic. The sultan was chosen from among the senior officers of the army, usually as the result of a *coup d'état* or other form of struggle between rival commanders. In 1260, Qutuz, a Mameluke army officer, was sultan.

As soon as they heard that Hulagu had left for Mongolia, the Mamelukes decided to fight. The battle took place on 3 September 1260 at Ain Jaloot, ten miles south/southeast of Nazareth. The Mongols were defeated and their commander Kitbugha was killed. Qutuz marched on to Damascus and announced the annexation of Syria to Egypt. Al Nasir Yusuf, the former Ayoubid King of Syria, had been captured by the Mongols and was subsequently executed. On the return march to Egypt, Qutuz was murdered by Baybers, one of his own officers, who thereby himself became sultan.

The arrival of the Mongols had further divided the Crusaders against one another. The Prince of Antioch became their ally, the people of Acre helped the Mamelukes to fight Kitbugha. The Templars declared their support for Egypt, whereat the Hospitallers advocated an alliance with Hulagu. Syria and Egypt, however, were not saved solely by the fighting power of the Mamelukes, but by the fact that the Mongols fell out among themselves. The descendants of Jenghis Khan disputed the supreme power and wore themselves out in civil wars on the steppes.

The Crusaders were now so weak and so divided against themselves, that they were no longer able to put an army in the field. The enthusiasm which had inspired the early Crusaders had evaporated and many of them were solely preoccupied with commerce and the export of oriental goods to the West.

From the point of view of the Mameluke Sultan of Egypt, the Crusaders no longer constituted a danger to the Muslim world, unless the Mongol invaders were to come back. Should they do so and the Crusaders join them, the alliance might be too strong for the Mameluke army. Baybers decided, therefore, that it would be wise to eliminate the Crusader states before the Mongols returned.

The Counts of Tripoli had become extinct and Tripoli had been united to the Princedom of Antioch. Richard Cœur de Lion during his Crusade had annexed Cyprus, which was now governed by the Lusignan dynasty. There were therefore now three Crusader states – the Kingdom of Cyprus, the Princedom of Antioch and Tripoli combined, and the so-called Kingdom of Jerusalem, with its capital at Acre, which in practice was governed by a commune of local notables.

In a series of whirlwind campaigns, from 1265 to 1268, Baybers captured Caesarea, Jaffa, Safad and then the great city of Antioch. The Prince of Antioch was left with Tripoli alone and the 'Kingdom of Jerusalem' was reduced to a small state consisting only of Acre, Haifa, Tyre, Sidon and Beirut.

In the spring of 1271, Baybers seemed to be about to march on Tripoli, when he heard of the arrival of Prince Edward of Cornwall, later King Edward I of England, who landed at Acre on 9 May 1271. Prince Edward had less than a thousand men and was not in a position to challenge Baybers to battle. However, he wrote to

Abagha Khan, the son of Hulagu, urging him to invade Syria and promising his cooperation.

The threat seems to have been sufficient to cause Baybers to change his plans and to sign a ten-year truce with Tripoli. On 16 June 1272 Prince Edward was stabbed by an assassin, allegedly sent by Baybers. It was on this occasion that the prince's life is said to have been saved by his wife Eleanor, who sucked the poison from his wound.

On 17 June 1277 Sultan Baybers was present at a reception in Damascus. One of the guests was an amir called Malik al Qahir, a descendant of the Ayoubids, of whom the Mamelukes had originally been slaves. Malik al Qahir made the mistake of being popular and had aroused the jealousy of the sultan, who invited him to join him for a drink. Baybers had placed poison in the amir's cup but, in a moment of absent-mindedness, he drank it himself and died three days later. Baybers was a man of towering personality and tireless energy and was the real founder of the Mameluke Empire. He inflicted mortal wounds on the Crusaders although he did not live to administer the *coup de grâce*.

After an interval of instability during which rival claimants manœuvred to seize the throne, Baybers was succeeded by Qalaun, a Mameluke commander almost as capable and as ruthless as himself. Hulagu had meanwhile assumed the title of Il Khan and had carved out an empire for himself, consisting of Persia, Iraq, Armenia, and Asia Minor, with Tabriz as the capital. The River Euphrates was the boundary between the Mongols of Persia and the Mameluke Empire of Syria and Egypt, as it had been between Rome and the Parthians. In September 1280, a Mongol force crossed the Euphrates and laid waste the province of Aleppo. In 1281, a larger army invaded Syria and a pitched battle was fought between them and the Mamelukes under Qalaun, near Homs, on 30 October 1281. The Mongols were driven back across the Euphrates.

Syria and Palestine had now returned to the unhappy situation which they had endured in the past – the cockpit for the struggle between a Mongol military empire in Iraq and Persia, on the one hand, and a similar military régime in Egypt on the other. In the same manner the Syro-Palestine causeway had been the scene of the endless wars between the Assyrian-Babylonian Empires and the Pharaohs, and between the Seleucids of Antioch and the Ptolemies of Egypt.

Before marching against the Mongols near Homs, Qalaun had concluded a ten-year truce with the Crusader states to avoid the danger of their joining the Mongols. Once the latter were defeated, however, he no longer saw any need to conciliate the Crusaders. Unscrupulously breaking the truce, he captured the Hospitallers' great frontier fortress of Crac des Chevaliers, still today one of the most impressive buildings in Syria. Then, on 26 April 1289, again in violation of the truce, he carried Tripoli by assault.

The remnant of the Crusaders were now in desperate straits, holding only a strip of coastline from Acre to Beirut. Venice, which derived large profits from trade with Acre, sent a rabble of untrained Italian levies to defend the city. Receiving no pay, these mercenaries soon became mutinous. One morning in August 1290, they sud-denly sallied out and began to massacre and rob the Arab inhabi-tants of the neighbouring villages. This outrage provided Sultan Qalaun with a useful pretext for the final extermination of the Crusader states. He immediately ordered the mobilization of the Mameluke army, but before he could lead it to Palestine, he died on 10 November 1290.

Sultan Khalil, the son of Qalaun, led his father's army to the siege of Acre. The attackers were ten times as numerous as the defenders and disposed of the heaviest siege train ever yet used in war. By bombardment and by driving mine galleries beneath the walls, several large breaches were made. On 18 May 1291 the Mamelukes advanced at dawn and swarmed up the breaches. The Crusaders, especially the Templars and Hospitallers, fought on desperately until three o'clock in the afternoon, by which time the greater part of them had been killed, and the Mamelukes poured into the town. In the ensuing few weeks the remaining fortresses on the coast were abandoned. After 194 years, the Crusading wars in Palestine and Syria came to an end, although the Kingdom of Cyprus was to survive for a further two hundred years.

In 1295, Ghazan, a great grandson of Hulagu and an extremely capable ruler, mounted the throne of the Mongol Il Khans of Persia. He immediately announced his conversion to Islam. The whole of his army was 'converted' on the same day. Thenceforward the wars between Mamelukes and Mongols were no longer wars of religion, both sides being Muslims.

Ghazan Khan invaded Syria in 1299 and completely defeated the Mameluke army at Wadi al Khazindar near Homs. Once again panic swept Damascus. But Ghazan was a Muslim and claimed to be a civilized ruler. Damascus was occupied without a massacre but when the conquerors were preparing to annex Syria, reports arrived that another Mongol army had invaded Persia, obliging Ghazan to march back. Once again Mongol civil wars had arrested the progress of their conquests. Thereafter the Il Khan dynasty of Persia fell into decline and they did not again invade Syria.

The Golden Age of the Mameluke Sultans of Egypt was the reign of the great Sultan al Nasir Muhammad, from 1293 to 1341. The Mameluke régime had now no serious enemy. The Mongol Il Khans of Persia were in decline and the Crusaders had been exterminated. The Mameluke Empire was based on Egypt, extended to Mecca and Medina in Arabia, and included Syria and Palestine and the province of Cilicia in Asia Minor. The destruction of the Crusader ports of Acre, Tripoli and Antioch had channelled all the oriental trade through Alexandria, and Egypt was rich and prosperous.

Syria and Palestine likewise benefited from the security which they always enjoyed when they formed part of a powerful empire, instead of being a cockpit for rival powers. The Mameluke system, it is true, gave rise to periodic civil wars between rival military commanders, but these were fought out between opposing Mameluke factions and did not greatly affect the Syrians.

The Mameluke régime was one of the most extraordinary in history. The Mamelukes were a ruling military class, depending on an army which consisted solely of Turkish ex-slaves. Neither Syrians nor Egyptians were eligible for enlistment. All Mamelukes had to be born on the steppes of central Asia and to arrive in Syria as slave boys. The sons of Mamelukes born to them in Egypt or Syria were considered to be inferior and were not accepted in regular Mameluke regiments.

The fact that all Mamelukes had to be reared in the cold northern climate of the steppes ensured an endless supply of new blood. The sultan was chosen after a struggle between rival claimants brought up in the nomadic tribes of the north, all of whom had then worked their way up through the army from slave to sultan. This system produced a succession of rulers of outstanding courage and determination, not to say ferocity.

Although the ruling class were Turks, who rarely learned to speak Arabic and regarded the Syrians as inferiors, they were nevertheless wise enough to make use of their services. In the fourteenth century, the Syrians were still as civilized as any nation in the world and both Egypt and Syria possessed a well-trained civil service and an administration inherited from the Romans, the Byzantines and the Arab caliphs. The commercial community was also both wealthy and competent. The Mamelukes took advantage of the skill of the government officials and the men of business. Although they did not enlist them, they employed Syrians in important administrative posts, received them at the palace and bestowed upon them titles and honours.

Until 1382, the Mameluke sultans had been Turks from the tribes of the steppes. In that year, however, the supreme power was seized by a Mameluke called Barqooq who was a Circassian, a member of a race which lived in the Caucasus and was distinct from the Turks. The régime thereafter underwent considerable modification, nearly all subsequent sultans being Circassians. The latter were less despotic, they gave their Mamelukes a good education and learned to speak Arabic. They were, however, also less martial than their predecessors and under them the army gradually deteriorated.

The Mameluke Empire lasted altogether for 267 years, from 1250 to 1517, during which period it attained an extraordinary degree of power and magnificence, and was one of the world's greatest states. The splendour of the empire, however, was achieved by considerable oppression and over-taxation, especially in Egypt.

97

Both the good and the evil effect of the Mameluke régime were less extreme in Syria than in Egypt. The thriving ports of Acre, Tyre, Tripoli and Antioch, which had been so wealthy in Crusader times, were destroyed by Baybers and Qalaun and the transit trade thereafter passed through Egypt alone. On the other hand, the Syrians, though they lived in fear of the Mongols, were less over-taxed and oppressed than were the Egyptians.

In Trans-Jordan and eastern Syria, the armed, nomadic tribes remained largely independent. It must, moreover, never be forgotten that Syria owed to the martial prowess of the Mamelukes her escape from destruction by the Mongols.

The years from 1305 to 1399 passed peacefully in Syria in so far as external enemies were concerned. The Mongol Il Khans of Persia and Iraq were in decline, and in 1334 the dynasty came to an end and the empire split into several small states. Asia Minor, most of which had been tributary to the Il Khans, was also divided up into more than twenty little Turkish amirates. There was no government in the north or the east strong enough to invade Syria and challenge the Mameluke Empire.

Internally, however, the situation was less satisfactory. The Circassian Mamelukes were less autocratic than their Turkish predecessors and control was relaxed throughout the empire. The great amirs still remained rich but the weakening authority of the government resulted in the reduction of the state finances to the verge of bankruptcy. The usual expedients – higher and higher taxes and depreciation of the currency – only aggravated the disease. The general disintegration of the régime resulted in unending *coups d'état*, and every two or three years the sultan was deposed and replaced by another. Successive viceroys of Damascus rebelled against the sultan in Cairo, giving rise to frequent civil wars.

Nature seemed intent on adding to the confusion created by man. Periods of famine due to lack of rain or the failure of the seasonal rise of the Nile seem to have been more frequent than usual. A succession of earthquakes inflicted great damage on the cities of Syria. Worse still were the epidemics of bubonic plague which, in 1348, spread to

Europe also, where it was known as the Black Death. Syria and Egypt, however, suffered frequent visitations of the plague throughout the fourteenth and the fifteenth centuries. Between fifteen and twenty epidemics are recorded in the course of two hundred years. Contemporary historians estimate that the population of Egypt and Syria were reduced by these calamities to one-third of their former numbers.

Nevertheless, we need not form too black a picture of this period. Many merchants were rich and lived in splendid town mansions. The disasters of plague, poverty and famine still fell largely on the poor, particularly on the Egyptian fellaheen. The country population of Syria and Palestine were more independent and more warlike, and were assisted in resisting oppression by their deserts and mountains.

In spite of the general political decline Syria remained one of the most civilized countries in the world. Free hospitals were available in most of the great cities, and as physicians, surgeons and oculists, the Syrians were probably still as good as any in existence. The only other countries which at this period produced scientists, astronomers and mathematicians were the Byzantine Empire, and Muslim Spain, with Sicily and southern Italy but little behind them. All these except the Byzantine Empire owed their scientific knowledge to previous Arab rule.

The most terrible single disaster which overtook Syria during the period of Mameluke decline was the invasion of Tamerlane. The descendants of Jenghis Khan had fallen into decline and the Il Khanate of Persia had disappeared when Tamerlane rose to power. A member of a semi-agricultural tribe of Turkish origin in Transoxiana, he was to prove as savage and sadistic a conqueror as Jenghis Khan. In 1370 he made himself master of Transoxiana. In the period from then to 1396, he overran all Persia and Iraq and, on two occasions, carried his victorious armies into what is now southern Russia, reaching the Ural Mountains and devastating the basins of the Don and the Volga. In 1398–9, he invaded India, and captured and destroyed Delhi, carrying untold wealth to Samarqand, which he made his capital.

During these years, he had not interfered with Syria, which was ruled at the time by the first of the Circassian sultans, the capable Barqooq. When, however, he returned to Samarqand in 1399 after the destruction of Delhi, he received information of the death of Sultan Barqooq and the succession of his feeble son Faraj who was still a boy ten years old. The Cairo government was torn by the intrigues of rival amirs and the viceroy of Damascus was in rebellion. The whole Mameluke Empire was in confusion.

In November 1399, Tamerlane left Samarqand and marched to Tabriz in northern Persia. In August 1400, he took Sivas, which, however, did not belong to the Mameluke Empire. He then moved to the northern frontier of Syria, whence he sent a message to Cairo demanding the acknowledgment of his suzerainty and the payment of tribute. The messenger, however, was executed by being cut in half at the waist. On 15 September 1400 news reached Cairo that Tamerlane had taken Malatia on the northern frontier of Syria. A meeting was called in Cairo to decide on the action to be taken but the rival amirs were unable to agree and nothing was done.

In October 1400, Tamerlane marched on Aleppo. The Mameluke garrison of Syria concentrated outside the city and, on 30 October, a pitched battle took place in which the Mamelukes were utterly defeated. In the confusion after the battle, Tamerlane carried Aleppo by storm and the sack of the city lasted four days. Every male, regardless of age, was massacred while the women and girls were rounded up, stripped and handed over to the troops for their amusement. The heads of those killed were built into towers of skulls all round the city. A few days later Hama also was taken and the same scenes repeated.

The news of the sack of Aleppo reached Cairo on 8 November 1400. Not, however, until 8 December did the Mameluke army leave Cairo, reaching Damascus on 23 December. Three days later Tamerlane's army arrived. Bypassing the city, it camped at Qatana, fourteen miles to the southwest. An indecisive action ensued and the two armies remained facing one another until 8 January 1401. On that day a rumour reached the Mameluke commanders to the effect that a group of rival amirs were planning a *coup d'état* in Cairo.

Taking the young sultan with them, they left the army secretly by night and rode as fast as they could for Cairo.

The Mameluke army, finding that it had been deserted by its senior officers, disbanded itself, leaving Damascus to its fate. Tamerlane, however, who did not wish to engage in a costly siege, sent for the notables of the city and declared to them that he was himself a pious Muslim and that he had decided to spare Damascus 'for the sake of the Companions of the Prophet who had dwelt there'. The notables, immensely relieved, agreed to open the gates.

No sooner, however, were Tamerlane's troops inside the city than he changed his tune. A general massacre ensued, many of the victims being tortured with refinements of cruelty. All the women were collected and raped. The sack of Damascus lasted for nineteen days. Before leaving, Tamerlane caused the city to be set on fire in several places. As a strong wind was blowing, the greater part of Damascus was destroyed including the great mosque of the Umayyads.

During the period from 1300 to 1400, a new Muslim Empire had been building up in Asia Minor and the Balkans. Founded by a small Turkman chief called Othman, it came to be known as the Othmanli, a name corrupted in Europe to Ottoman. On 20 July 1402 Tamerlane completely defeated the Ottoman army at Ankara and overran the whole of Asia Minor. Thence he sent another emissary to Cairo to demand instant submission. The trembling Mameluke amirs hastened to comply, the name and titles of Tamer-lane were included in the Friday prayers, coins were minted in Cairo in his name and a humble embassy was sent to the Conqueror, bearing rich presents and an undertaking to pay tribute.

Although Tamerlane was now nearly seventy years old, he decided to conquer China. But, old campaigner as he was, his strength at length gave way and he died on the steppes of Turkestan on 18 February 1405. The world from the Balkans to Delhi breathed again. After a few years of confusion, he was succeeded by his son Shah Rukh, who proved to be a man of peace.

After the death of Tamerlane, the Mamelukes recovered some-thing of their prestige. Shattered by the Conqueror, the Ottoman

Empire needed some years to recover and the descendants of Tamerlane were weak and divided. The Mameluke Sultans Shaikh
al-Mahmoodi (1412–21), Barsbay (1422–38) and Jaqmaq (1438–
53) ruled with wisdom and moderation, and Syria enjoyed a period
of peace.

The nature of the régime itself had changed profoundly under the
Circassian sultans. Military discipline had been relaxed and the
amirs and sultans had become interested in politics rather than in
war, which had been the chief preoccupation of the great Turkish
Mamelukes like Baybers and Qalaun. Corruption increased and
even the army became inefficient. After the death of Sultan Jaqmaq
in 1453, a series of incompetent rulers followed one another in rapid
succession. Between 1453 and 1516, a period of sixty-three years,
twelve Mameluke sultans mounted the throne, an average of just
over five years for each reign. None of them were of any distinction
except perhaps Qaitbay, who ruled from 1468 to 1495.

Meanwhile the Ottoman Empire had recovered from its defeat by
Tamerlane, and, in 1453, had captured Constantinople from the
last Byzantine emperor. Once more the Ottomans were expanding
in every direction. Persia, too, was in the process of revival under the
Safavid dynasty. Of the old régimes, the Seljuqs and the Mongols
had vanished. Only the Mameluke Empire, now 236 years old,
still survived. In 1486, fighting actually broke out between the
Ottomans and the Mamelukes in Cilicia but soon afterwards the
Ottomans became more concerned with the rise of Safavid Persia.

At the beginning of the sixteenth century, the Ottoman Empire
was virile, energetic and up to date, particularly in the military field.
The Ottomans were the first to realize the immense power of the
newly invented firearms. To capture Constantinople in 1453,
Muhammad II, the Conqueror, used greater masses of artillery and
bigger guns than the world had ever seen. Soon the Janissaries,
originally archers, were re-armed with handguns. No European
army was so up to date.

In 1512, the Ottoman Sultan Salim I, surnamed the Grim,
marched against the Safavid Ismail Shah who, in 1508, had
occupied Iraq. Shah Ismail was of the Shiite division of Islam, the

Ottoman sultan a Sunni, and religious hatred was added to political rivalry. The two imperial adversaries met in a pitched battle at Chaldiran in eastern Asia Minor, near Lake Urmia. The Persians had virtually no firearms and were heavily defeated by the Ottomans with their more modern weapons.

The Mamelukes had originated from the steppes of central Asia. The finest horsemen on earth, they proved themselves invincible on horseback with lance, sword and bow. But the corollary of their prowess as cavalry was that they despised all other methods of warfare. Mamelukes refused to fight on foot, or to go to sea, tasks which, when they became necessary, had to be performed by inferior troops whom the Mamelukes regarded with contempt.

When the invention of firearms made the formation of artillery and infantry essential, the whole military system of the Mamelukes was challenged. They consented to use cannon in sieges, a form of operation in which cavalry had never been of much value. But they bitterly opposed the use of firearms or artillery in battle, denouncing such methods as contrary to military honour.

As soon as he had defeated Ismail Shah, the Ottoman Sultan Salim I turned on the Mamelukes. The two armies met in battle at Marj Dabiq, north of Aleppo, on 24 August 1516. The Mamelukes, resplendent in magnificent uniforms and superbly mounted, consisted almost entirely of cavalry. The Ottomans brought on to the field a numerous artillery and the Janissary infantry, armed with handguns.

The Mameluke Sultan Qansuh al Ghori, a veteran of seventyfive years of age, fought most bravely but the disparity in weapons, training and discipline could not be atoned for by courage alone. Qansuh died on the field and the Mameluke army was utterly defeated.

The Ottomans took over Syria and Palestine without encountering any further opposition. In October 1516, Damascus was occupied. The Ottomans marched on to Egypt and on 22 January 1517 again completely defeated the Mamelukes outside Cairo.

Syria and Palestine were to remain under Ottoman rule for exactly four centuries – from 1516 to 1916, when the British army advancing

from Egypt and the rebel Arabs under the Amir Feisal of the
Hejaz, set about the task of their eviction.

KEY DATES

1220–5	Destruction of Persia by Jenghis Khan
1260	Invasion of Syria by Hulagu, grandson of Jenghis Khan
3 September 1260	Battle of Ain Jaloot, Mongols repulsed from Syria
1268	Destruction of Antioch by Sultan Baybers
1291	Final extermination of the Crusader states
1299	Capture of Damascus and subsequent withdrawal of the Mongols under Ghazan Khan
1293–1341	Reign of Sultan al Nasir Muhammad, the Golden Age of the Mameluke Empire
1382	Replacement of Turkish by Circassian sultans
1305–99	Syria at peace under the Mamelukes
1401	Sack of Damascus by Tamerlane
1405	Death of Tamerlane
1401–1516	Syria at peace under the Mamelukes but deteriorating economically
1512	Defeat of Ismail Shah of Persia by the Ottoman Sultan Salim the Grim
24 August 1516	Battle of Marj Dabiq
October 1516	Ottoman occupation of Damascus
1517	Annexation of Syria and Egypt to the Ottoman Empire

7 Syria under the Ottoman Empire: 1517–1909

FROM THE CAPTURE OF CAIRO by the Ottomans in 1517 until the British invasion of Palestine in 1917, Syria and Palestine remained remote and half-neglected provinces of the Ottoman Empire.[5]

Sultan Salim The Grim remained a few months in Cairo after his overthrow of the Mamelukes and then returned to Istanbul. The Ottoman Empire reached the height of its glory under his son, Sulaiman the Magnificent, better known in the Middle East as Sulaiman the Lawgiver (1520–66). Although in his reign, the empire returned to its traditional pre-occupation with Europe, an attempt was made to maintain an administration in the Arab provinces.

In Kerak, for example, a pasha[6] was appointed as governor with a commandant of troops and a qadhi or judge. Set amid a remote and unfriendly population, the officials apparently considered that their best chance of survival was to become identified with the Arabs and to forget Istanbul. The governor accordingly declared his independence. As the cost of a punitive expedition would have been considerable, the Sublime Porte[7] had recourse to guile. A senior pasha was sent to Syria and invited the governor of Kerak to a conference at which he was kidnapped and sent to Istanbul. Thereafter, however, the Ottomans abandoned the attempt to administer Trans-Jordan.

At the present day, three small sub-tribes exist in the Kerak district. The Bashabsha are said to be the descendants of the rebellious pasha (pronounced by the local Arabs Basha), the

Aghawat the progeny of the commandant of troops and the Qudhat the posterity of the qadhi. Thus did the outposts of empire melt away into the hills of Moab.

It is difficult entirely to account for the inefficiency of the Ottoman régime. We, in the twentieth century, think of the Ottoman Empire as hopelessly out of date, and such was indeed its condition for the last two hundred years of its existence. But in 1517, the Ottoman army at least was well in advance of its European contemporaries. In spite of this fact, however, the replacement of the Mameluke by the Ottoman régime seems to have resulted in an immediate deterioration in the standards of government in Syria and Palestine.

The following considerations may at least partly account for the four centuries of neglect and misrule experienced by Syria and Palestine under the Ottomans.

1 The original background of the Ottoman Empire had been one of Muslim Holy War. The first hundred years of the growth of the state, 1288–1388 had been solely devoted to war against Christians in southeast Europe. Not until 1392 did expansion commence against Muslims in Asia. With occasional interruptions – the wars with Tamerlane, with Ismail Shah and with the Mamelukes – the principal efforts of the Ottomans throughout their history were devoted to hostilities against the Christians of Europe.

As a result of this historical background, the ethos of the Ottoman state, founded on holy war, was divided between war and religion. For 250 years, say from 1430 to 1680, the Ottoman army was perhaps the finest in the world. But this concentration on militarism resulted in a contemptuous attitude towards commerce, industry and learning. Great empires can only be maintained by states with ample financial resources, such as only industry and commerce can produce.

2 The basis of the imperial government was the despotism of the sultan. Moreover, in order to avoid any chance of civil war by rival claimants to the throne, the heir apparent was often kept virtually under house arrest until his father died and he himself ascended the throne. Thus the man upon whose capacity to govern the future of the empire was to depend mounted the throne without any experi⁄ence or knowledge of government.

3 For thousands of years, Syria and Palestine had been at the very heart of the civilized world. In Old Testament times, they had lain between the great empires of Assyria and Egypt. Syria had been one of the most civilized and important provinces of the Persian and of the Roman Empires. She had been the seat of the Seleucid Empire from 301 to 133 BC. Damascus had, for ninety years, been the capital of the Umayyad Empire. During the rule of the Abbasid caliphs in Baghdad, Syria had been second only to Iraq. Through‑out the 350 years of the Ayoubid and Mameluke Empires, Syria had been second only to Egypt as part of a Great Power. After the Ottoman conquest, however, not only was Syria distant from Istanbul (Constantinople) but the preoccupation of the Ottoman Empire with its wars against the European Powers condemned Syria and Palestine to neglect.

4 One cause of the decay and impoverishment of Syria, Palestine and Egypt under the Ottomans cannot, however, be imputed to governmental neglect. The Cape of Good Hope route to India and the Far East was discovered in 1497 by Vasco da Gama. In the past, as we have seen, much of the prosperity of Egypt and Syria had been due to the oriental trade route which crossed these countries. Hence‑forward the products of India, Indonesia and China were carried in great sailing ships round the Cape. Commercially Syria suddenly became a backwater.

The Ottoman system of government in the Arab countries was in general to maintain a large military garrison and a staff of civil officials in the principal cities, such as Damascus or Aleppo. Within a distance of five, ten or twenty miles of the town, the government was in full control and taxes were regularly collected. Beyond that distance, taxes were only fitfully paid and the roads were unsafe. In areas still further away, tribal chiefs were in control, virtually independent but paying occasional lip service to the authorities.

Now and again when tribal lawlessness passed all bounds, a large military force was sent out as a punitive column. If the tribes were defeated, which did not always happen, their villages were burned, their encampments plundered and their cattle and sheep driven off by the troops. Perhaps the tribes would then submit and promise not to do it again – or at least not until next time.

One of the most disastrous aspects of Ottoman policy towards the tribes was the frequent use of deceit. Tribal chiefs were constantly lured into meetings with government officials, cordially welcomed and feasted and then suddenly arrested, loaded with chains and sent to Istanbul to be put to death. Such measures destroyed all hope of cooperation between the tribes and the government.

The Syrian desert east of Damascus and of the Dead Sea consisted of rolling steppes on which grew grass and shrubs suitable as grazing for camels and sheep. The desert tribes or bedouins, mounted on camels, spent much of their time raiding one another and had thus preserved their hardihood and martial qualities. The weakness of the government enabled these tribal chiefs to dominate a great part of eastern Syria and Trans-Jordan, ruling as semi-independent princes. If the government collected a large military force to chastise them, the bedouins mounted their camels and vanished into the desert. It is remarkable that the Turks never seem to have had any desire to penetrate the desert, a task which long fascinated adventurous Europeans.

When the tribes were nearly always out of control, town dwellers were afraid to go far afield and relied on the Ottoman authorities for their safety. At the same time, while large Ottoman garrisons occupied the great cities, many officials, officers and soldiers inevitably married locally. Some remained after their discharge from the army and raised families. By this means, city dwellers became to a considerable extent Ottomanized, both in sentiment and by intermarriage.

As a result of the Russo-Turkish War of 1877, certain provinces in the Caucasus were surrendered by the Ottoman government to Russia. Many of the Muslim inhabitants migrated rather than submit to Christian rule. Acting on the old principle of 'divide and rule', the Sublime Porte resettled some of these displaced communities in Syria and Trans-Jordan in the more turbulent Arab areas. Surrounded by the hostile Arab population, the Circassians could be relied upon to support Ottoman authority: Circassians still play an influential role in Syria and Jordan.

The tribes and the rural population, however, were little affected by such foreign immigration, just as they had remained unaffected in classical times when the cities were largely populated by Greeks. The Ottomans themselves were by no means racially pure Turks. During their early conquests in the Balkans, they had become mixed with Greeks, Serbians, Slavs, Bulgarians and many other races.

The consequence of the continuance of this state of affairs for four centuries was to divide the populations of Syria and Palestine into three classes more or less inimical to one another.

1 The city dwellers were strong supporters of the government, which represented such law and order as existed. The urban population was also to a considerable extent intermarried with Ottoman soldiers and officials. The townspeople regarded the tribes with fear and aversion.

2 The agricultural population constituted the second class. On the coastal plains of Palestine and in the vicinity of garrison towns the government was able to control the cultivators, who suffered a good deal of exploitation and oppression and were inclined to become somewhat servile.

Further from garrison towns, however, the cultivators retained their martial spirit, and frequently resisted the government, refused to pay taxes and fought the army, the gendarmerie or one another.

3 The third element of the population was the nomads of the desert, who were extremely martial. As the bedouins fought against the government and also raided the cultivators, they were hated by townsmen and farmers alike.

To a great extent, the population is still divided into the same three groups.

The Ottoman security forces in Arab countries were divided into two services, the city police and the gendarmerie, a mounted force armed with rifles, who operated in rural areas. This gendarmerie at times behaved with considerable arrogance. If a party of gendarmes arrived at a village, they would immediately demand a meal. If the food were delayed, they would apply their canes freely to any villagers they could catch. In the same spirit, if the meal were not to their satisfaction, they would demand more or tip all the dishes on to the floor and order their hosts to sweep up the mess and cook a fresh meal. If they came to investigate a crime, they would seize and flog the first villagers they met, as the quickest way of obtaining information.

It is perhaps not surprising that the security forces were sometimes welcomed with bullets. At the same time, however, it must be admitted that many junior Ottoman officials, stationed with an escort of a dozen ragged gendarmes in some remote tribal area, maintained some semblance of government authority by the sheer force of their personalities in a quite extraordinary manner.

It is, moreover, to be noted that these gendarmes and minor officials were probably themselves natives of the country – Arabs we should call them, although before the First World War people did not think in terms of Turks and Arabs. The authorities believed that such autocratic methods were the only way to maintain government authority. Even the tribes seemed to regard this state of affairs as natural. Moreover, on both sides, this mentality lasted well into the postwar period, when the governments were supposed to be 'Arab', and much of it remains today.

The present writer well remembers, in the 1920s, talking to an old Arab farmer, sitting on the ground making coffee on a little fire of sticks. When the conversation turned on Arab government, he shook his head thoughtfully. 'You can't make a pasha out of an Arab,' he said, 'any more than you can make a fire-tongs out of a piece of wood.' Unaware that Arabs had once ruled an empire extending from Spain to China, the situation with which he was familiar seemed to him to be only natural. Whatever the government was, he was against it, but it never occurred to him to aspire to replace it.

One of my closest colleagues and contemporaries was an officer who came of an old Damascus family which had been closely identified with Ottoman rule. Before the First World War, he had been a junior officer in the Turkish army. After the war, of course, he found himself an 'Arab', yet he never lost his original mentality and frequently explained to me that 'Arabs cannot be ruled except with a big stick'. Thus the town dwellers of today have retained something of the contempt which they learned from the Turks towards the rural population.

Our own civilization has today become predominantly urban. Moreover, we admire law and order and are guided in forming our opinions of past civilizations by the writings left by the authors of the time. We, therefore, tend to praise the Greeks and the Romans, who enforced public security and whose rule was based on cities. In doing so, we are apt to forget that these urban régimes were based on the slavery or the serfdom of the agricultural population.

In a sense, the Ottoman régime may have been a relatively happy one for the rural Arabs, who formed a majority of the population and many of whom, though they lived amidst violence and blood/shed, were able to feel themselves free men. The Ottomans were ready enough to oppress them but fortunately did not often have the power to do so. Our present obsession with race renders us unconscious of these tensions. To us, everyone in Syria is an Arab and thus they must obviously all be happy together.

Yet in spite of the frequent outbreaks of violence in Ottoman times, gleams of Arab humour often lighten the narrative of these turbulent incidents. In the 1850s, for example, the Ottoman governor of Nablus decided to collect taxes from the Adwan tribe west of Amman. When he entered the tribal area, with an escort of a squadron of cavalry, he was met by the chief, Ali ibn Adwan, and several hundred Arabs on horseback.

Bowing low to show his profound respect, the shaikh asked permission for his men to show their delight at His Excellency's condescension in visiting his servants. His Excellency having kindly signified his consent, several hundred tribal horsemen rode down upon him at full gallop, screaming wildly and firing their rifles in the air. On reaching the visitors, they wheeled their horses and raced madly round and round him, still firing in the air and screaming. 'Thank you, thank you, that is enough,' said the pasha, slightly alarmed. 'We have not yet shown sufficient honour to Your Excellency,' bowed Shaikh Ali, at the same time yelling to his followers, 'Hot it up, boys! Show the pasha how honoured we are by his visit'.

'Stop them! Stop them, for God's sake!' shouted the governor. 'Show His Excellency how much we love him,' yelled Ali ibn Adwan. By this time the governor's horse was out of control and he had lost one of his stirrups. The cavalry squadron was in confusion and several of their horses had bolted. The pasha decided that discretion was the better part of valour and, turning bridle, galloped off with more speed than dignity for Nablus. Behind him rode the hospitable shaikh, calling out in stentorian tones, 'We were honoured by Your Excellency's visit.'

Lebanon formed something of an exception to this pattern, because the mountains made punitive operations difficult and because most of the inhabitants were not Muslims but either Christians or Druzes. In southern Lebanon there were large communities of Shiites and in the mountains east of Tripoli were Nusairis, both regarded by the Ottomans as Muslim heretics. It was, of course, the impassability of the mountains which had induced these dissident religious communities to seek refuge there.

After the conquest of Egypt, Salim the Grim recognized Fakhr al Din al Mani as paramount chief of Lebanon with a considerable measure of autonomy. His grandson, Fakhr al Din II, ruled Lebanon from 1590 to 1635, during which he built up a considerable state which included the coast from Beirut to Haifa, the province of Galilee and even Nablus and Ajlun, now in Jordan. In 1633, however, the sultan decided that the Amir Fakhr al Din had become too powerful. A large army was sent against him, overran Lebanon and carried Fakhr al Din in chains to Istanbul.

Ever since Phoenician days, Lebanon had looked west across the Mediterranean, rather than east to Arabia. Fakhr al Din II revived these ancient tendencies. He concluded a private commercial treaty with Florence, at the time ruled by the Medici family. He thereby took the first tentative step towards establishing contact between the

Arab countries and the West, severed since the end of the Crusades, 350 years earlier.

The Manis became extinct in 1697 and were succeeded as lords of Lebanon by the Shihabis, who were to retain their power until 1841. The most famous of the dynasty was Bashir II al Shihabi, who ruled from 1788 to 1840 and built himself a famous mountain palace at Bait al Din, which is still worthy of a visit. Ruling over a small country which nevertheless included among its people Maronite Christians, Druzes and Sunni and Shiite Muslims, the amirs of Lebanon were artists at concealing their real faith. Like Paul, they strove to be all things to all men. It is alleged that Bashir had a Muslim, a Christian and a Druze wife. There are still Shihabi amirs in Lebanon, some professing Islam and some Christianity and said to be descended from Bashir's different wives.

The Maronites were a Christian sect, perhaps descended from the Monothelites, who had been denounced as heretical by the Byzantines. Like many other persecuted minorities, they took refuge in the mountains of Lebanon. In 1584, however, a Maronite College was opened in Rome by Pope Gregory XIII. Here many leading Maronites from Lebanon received their education. Combined with the Westernizing influence of the Mani and Shihabi amirs, the Maronite College in Rome was to prove of great importance in the development of Lebanon, and indirectly of Syria also, by increasing the penetration of Western ideas. In 1736, the Maronites accepted the spiritual authority of the papacy.

As already indicated, the reign of Sulaiman the Magnificent (1520–66) marked the high noon of Ottoman glory and power, during which their armies annexed most of Hungary, unsuccessfully besieged Vienna and reached Ratisbon in Germany. Sulaiman, however, was succeeded by several weak sons, whose incompetence was increased by their virtual detention in the palace until they mounted the throne.

Under these circumstances, power tended to pass to the chief minister or Grand Wazir. At the end of the seventeenth century, the able Koprulu family temporarily retrieved the fortunes of the empire, passing the wazirate from father to son and attempting to introduce reforms. These and subsequent modernizing measures, however, rarely if ever penetrated to so remote a province as Syria.

In conclusion, it may be noted that, although considerable areas of Syria and Palestine were often out of government control, there was never any question of overthrowing the Ottoman Empire or even of obtaining independence. The Ottomans were unable to administer or police rural districts, largely perhaps because Istanbul was not particularly interested in these remote areas. But the government maintained large garrisons in the great cities and the Arab tribes were incapable of cooperating with one another. The sultan, moreover, drew the loyalty of Muslims as the only great Islamic ruler in a world increasingly dominated by Christians.

So much for the internal affairs of Syria and Palestine under the Ottomans. A few words may be added on the subject of foreign intervention. After the Ottoman Conquest in 1517, the outside world made virtually no attempt to intervene in Syria or Palestine for nearly three hundred years. Ever since the first dawn of history, Syria had occupied the centre of the civilized stage. Placed half-way between Babylonia and Egypt, Rome and Persia, Constantinople and Baghdad, she had played for four thousand years the role of the bridge between East and West. Then, suddenly, from about 1500 onwards, she found herself a neglected and stagnant backwater.

For the first time, leadership was passing to the West. The young rising nations of western Europe were looking elsewhere. The Portuguese, the Dutch and then the British were rounding the Cape of Good Hope and occupying India, Indonesia and East Africa. In the West, Spain, France and England were engrossed in the conquest and development of America. This was the first occasion since the beginning of history that great international events were taking place in which Syria played no part.

In 1798, the West suddenly burst into the Middle East when Napoleon Bonaparte landed in Egypt and subsequently invaded Palestine. From 21 March to 20 May 1799 the French besieged Acre in vain, the town being held by Ahmad Pasha al Jazzár, assisted by an English fleet under Sir Sidney Smith. The confusion prevailing in Syria at the time is illustrated by the fact that Ahmad Pasha al Jazzár (The Butcher) was an escaped slave boy of Bosnian origin, who by intrigue, murder and civil war had made himself governor of Syria and Palestine.

Meanwhile a new and fanatical Muslim sect called the Wahhabis had appeared in central Arabia, under the leadership of the family of Saud. In May 1803, the Wahhabis had taken Mecca. In 1810, a force of six thousand men on camels burst into the province of Hauran, south of Damascus, and plundered thirty-five towns and villages, killing the male inhabitants. Damascus itself was in panic and the Wahhabis could probably have captured the city. Instead, however, they vanished into the desert with their loot. They continued to tax the eastern tribes from near Damascus to the vicinity of Aleppo, the Ottoman authorities being too weak to intervene.

In the confusion which followed Napoleon's invasion of Egypt, an Albanian soldier of fortune called Muhammad Ali had made himself dictator of that country. The Sublime Porte, unable to remove him, had recognized him as Pasha of Egypt, and had ordered him to drive Ibn Saud, the Wahhabi chief, from Mecca. In a three-year campaign, 1812–15, Muhammad Ali defeated Ibn Saud and suppressed the Wahhabis.

The sultan had thus successfully used the time-honoured policy of setting one thief to catch another. The Sublime Porte repeated the experiment in its attempts to crush the Greeks and, from 1824 to 1829, an army sent from Egypt fought in Greece. The sultan had promised Muhammad Ali the governorship of Syria in return for his help but ultimately refused to fulfil his pledge.

As a result, an Egyptian army commanded by Ibrahim Pasha, the son of Muhammad Ali, invaded Palestine and stormed Acre on 27 May 1832. The Amir Bashir al Shihabi, the ruler of Lebanon already mentioned, threw in his lot with Ibrahim Pasha. The latter marched through Syria in triumph, defeating the Ottoman army at Konia in Asia Minor, in December 1832. The Great Powers then intervened and, in May 1833, a convention was signed by which Syria was ceded to Muhammad Ali.

In 1839, however, the Ottomans invaded Syria but were again defeated by Ibrahim Pasha on 24 June 1839, at Nasib near Deraa, on the northern frontier of modern Jordan. The Great Powers again intervened and, in February 1841, new agreements were signed confining Muhammad Ali's rule to Egypt alone. Although the Syrians had at first welcomed Ibrahim Pasha with open arms, they quickly tired of his rule and when he was ultimately forced to withdraw, several revolts had already broken out.

In spite, however, of its ultimate failure, Ibrahim Pasha's invasion was instrumental in opening Syria, Lebanon and Palestine to Western influence. Muhammad Ali, who, it will be remembered, was an Albanian, had done much to introduce Western methods into Egypt, and owed his military victories to the fact that his regular army was trained on modern lines by French officers. During his nine-year occupation of Syria, Ibrahim Pasha, like his ally and contemporary in Lebanon, Bashir al Shihabi, had done what he could to introduce Western influence.

When the Ottomans resumed control of Syria and Palestine in 1840–1, Bashir escaped on a British ship to Malta. The Sublime Porte, realizing that military operations in the Lebanese mountains would be both costly and precarious, resorted to its normal policy of 'divide and rule' and set itself to stir up hatred between the Christians and the Druzes. The government was so far successful, that, in 1860, there were extensive massacres of the Christians by the Druzes.

Napoleon III, anxious to live up to Bonapartist tradition by gaining military victories, sent a French army to Lebanon where it remained for a year. The Powers of Europe again intervened and the sultan was obliged to agree to a convention whereby Lebanon was always to have a Christian governor approved of by the Western Powers. No Turkish troops were to be stationed in the area, the government of which was to enjoy a considerable measure of local autonomy, with direct access to Istanbul, independent of the Ottoman governor of Syria.

In Lebanon, however, greater influence was exercised by Western missionaries than by military force. The Jesuits had arrived as early as 1625. In 1734, in conjunction with the Maronites, they established the first modern school in any Arabic-speaking country.

In 1820, American Presbyterian missionaries landed in Beirut. Their activities, however, were confined to that town, which then contained only some nine thousand inhabitants. There were no local Protestants in the country and the Catholics and Maronites were almost as hostile to them as were the Muslims. The occupation of Syria by Ibrahim Pasha from 1832 to 1841, however, introduced a more liberal atmosphere, especially in education. The Americans were able to open schools, including one for girls, and to establish an Arabic printing press.

Even when, after nine years, Ibrahim Pasha was obliged to evacuate Syria and Palestine, the impetus given to education remained. By 1860, the Americans had spread to Jerusalem also and controlled a total of thirty-three schools. In 1866, they established in Beirut the Syrian Protestant College, later to become famous as the American University of Beirut. The rapid spread of the Protestant educational establishments spurred the Roman Catholics to increased efforts. They went even further afield and, in 1872, opened a school in Damascus and, in 1873, in Aleppo. The Jesuit Université de Saint Joseph opened in Beirut in 1875. Meanwhile, in 1860, the British Syrian Mission arrived and soon afterwards a Prussian Mission. It was through these institutions that modern Western ways of thought penetrated Syria. The most potent of these new ideas were nationalism and democracy.

From the political angle, one of the most important aspects of Western schools was that they taught in Arabic, a language neglected by the Ottomans. It was largely the revival of the study of Arabic literature, bringing to light the forgotten glories of Arab civilization in the days of the caliphs, which was ultimately to give rise to the demand for political emancipation from Ottoman rule. Ironically enough, the movement was begun by Lebanese Christians in Western-run schools.

Until 1918, however, Western educational efforts were almost limited to Lebanon and Palestine. East of the Lebanon and of the Jordan, education remained at a low ebb and it is probable that

117

some eighty-five per cent of the population were unable to read or write. In view of the fact that writing with an alphabet had actually been invented in these countries, some 2500 years before, the general illiteracy just before the First World War is a striking phenomenon.

Exactly how important the Arabic literary revival in Beirut really was is difficult to estimate. At any rate, throughout the remainder of the nineteenth century, it had no visible effect on the political scene. Meanwhile Abdul Hamid[8] II had become sultan in 1876 and was to retain the throne until 1909. The events of his long reign will be discussed in the next chapter.

KEY DATES

1517	Ottoman annexation of Syria
1517–1697	Domination of Lebanon by the Mani family
1520–66	Reign of Sulaiman the Magnificent, the high noon of Ottoman power
1799	Invasion of Palestine by Napoleon Bonaparte
1811	Seizure of power in Egypt by Muhammad Ali Pasha
1832–41	Invasion of Syria by Ibrahim Pasha, son of Muhammad Ali
1860–1	Occupation of Lebanon by the French under Napoleon III
1866	Establishment of the American Syrian Protestant College (later the American University of Beirut)
1876–1909	Reign of Ottoman Sultan Abdul Hamid II

8   Syria between the Wars:
1909–1939

IN THESE DEMOCRATIC DAYS, it has become fashionable to heap abuse on the autocracy of Abdul Hamid II, who ruled the Ottoman Empire from 1876 to 1909. The fact remains, however, that he was not unpopular with a great many Arabs.

The Balkans, it is true, were in a constant state of sedition, partly as the result of the activities of Russia and other Western Powers. The Arab provinces, however, for the most part remained quiet. It is true that there were frequent local disorders but these were produced by local grievances and were not inspired by any general aspirations to democracy or independence.

Arab loyalty was largely retained by the sultan by means of his religious propaganda, the vast majority of Arabs – perhaps even today – being in their heart of hearts more deeply moved by devotion to Islam than by national feeling. Pressed by the forces of nationalism imported from Europe, the policy of Abdul Hamid was to bind the empire together by loyalty to Islam. He took particular trouble to win the Arabs, the largest racial group in the empire, and to rouse their religious enthusiasm.

The discovery of the Cape of Good Hope route in 1497 had, as we have seen, transformed Syria and Egypt from the world's wealthiest markets into stagnant backwaters. The opening of the Suez Canal in 1869 restored to Egypt its international importance but not its wealth. Before 1497, the oriental merchandise had been landed in

Egypt, handled by Egyptian merchants and resold to European buyers. The Suez Canal merely permitted the passage of ships but Egyptian businessmen did not buy and resell the cargoes.

The advent of railways did something of the same kind for Syria and Iraq. Germany, a late arrival among the Great Powers of Europe, was seeking an outlet to the East and endeavoured to secure it by contracting with the Ottoman Empire to build a railway to Baghdad and Basra, at the head of the Persian Gulf.

The Ottoman Sultan Abdul Hamid (1876–1909) conceived the idea of extending his authority by building a similar railway from Damascus to Medina. A subsidiary line was constructed at the same time from Deraa to Haifa. (See map VII, page 210–11.) The constant Ottoman defeats and losses of territory in Europe as the result of pressure by Russia and Austria-Hungary had led the sultan, as we have seen, to woo the Arab provinces, neglected by the Sublime Porte for four centuries. The construction of the railway to Medina was partly paid for by pious contributions from Muslims outside the empire. On 12 April 1900 work commenced on the Hejaz Railway, beginning from the Damascus end. The sultan hoped that the railway would considerably strengthen his hold over the Arabs of Syria and Palestine.

The Turkish authorities had begun to spread their influence over Trans-Jordan in the 1880s. Their policy, however, was to collect taxes but not to attempt to prevent the tribes from fighting one another. Indeed, on the 'divide and rule' principle, the government at times encouraged inter-tribal wars. When the railway reached the Kerak district, an Ottoman governor was established there, supported by three battalions of infantry. In 1910, a rebellion broke out in Kerak but was crushed by the famous Sami Pasha, who had previously suppressed a revolt in the Jebel Druze. On the whole, the building of the railway was of benefit to Syria and Palestine and, if the First World War had not intervened, would have resulted in the establishment of Ottoman rule in Trans-Jordan.

Meanwhile outside influences were also affecting the Syrian situation. Nearly a century earlier, Muhammad Ali had seized power in Egypt and had opened up that country to Western influence. In 1882, the British had occupied it and had introduced a liberal political régime, allowing free discussion and a free press. Many Syrians with progressive views moved to Egypt to enjoy this more congenial atmosphere.

In an entirely different direction, Abdul Hamid gave rise to a tendency which has been the bane of many Arab countries ever since. Anxious to modernize his army the sultan had, in 1883, accepted a German military mission, which had among other activities instituted a system of military colleges for the training and education of officers. So efficient were these German-controlled institutions that Turkish army officers were soon better educated than most of their civilian contemporaries and more permeated with Western ideas. From this situation two results were to ensue:

(*a*) Firstly, young army officers became some of the leading political revolutionaries.

(*b*) Secondly, when the educational facilities available at military colleges came to be appreciated, many young men whose interests were intellectual rather than military, entered military colleges with a view to obtaining the best education available, although they had no great interest in a military career.

Although the independent Arab states of today look back upon the years of Ottoman rule with contempt and resentment, yet curious survivals of Turkish ways of thought still persist among them. One of these is the belief that high academic qualifications are the principal requisite in army officers. The result has been the same as in the Turkish army at the beginning of the century. The Arab armies tend to be over-staffed with intellectuals and political theorists, rather than with officers whose first interest lies in soldiering. Frequent military seizures of political power have resulted.

The stage was set for army intervention in politics in July 1908, when a military revolution broke out in the Turkish army, led by the young officers educated in the military colleges. Abdul Hamid was obliged to grant a constitution, abolish the censorship and release all political prisoners. An extraordinary wave of naïve

121

enthusiasm swept the empire, in Syria as elsewhere. Rich and poor, scholar and illiterate, Arab and Turk, assumed that the earthly paradise had arrived and embraced one another in the streets with delirious joy, crying *hurriya* – freedom.

In April 1909, as the result of an attempted counter-revolution, Abdul Hamid was dethroned and his brother Muhammad Reshad, a self-effacing figure, was made sultan in his stead. Thereafter power passed completely into the hands of the revolutionary party, the so-called Committee of Union and Progress (CUP), many of the leaders of which were young army officers.

But the earthly paradise soon faded from sight. In the very year of the 1908 revolution, Austria-Hungary annexed Bosnia and Herzegovina, two Ottoman provinces. Then Bulgaria seceded. In 1911, Italy invaded Libya. In 1912, a general war broke out in the Balkans. These were external disasters, but in their internal affairs the CUP were guilty of tragic blunders. In order to damp down the fires of nationalism, Abdul Hamid had insisted that all subjects of the empire were Ottomans and as such enjoyed complete equality. The CUP had carried out their revolution using this slogan, but once they were in power they seemed to lean to a policy of Turkish superiority, which appeared to treat the Arabs as a subject race. Thus, in the Arabic-speaking countries, the 1908 revolutionary en-thusiasm was quickly followed by a disillusioned revulsion of feeling.

In 1912, a political party was formed in Cairo consisting of Syrians, Lebanese and Palestinians, who were unable to carry out political propaganda in their own countries. The object of the party was to press for administrative decentralization, that is to say for autonomous governments in various Arab countries, using Arabic as their official language, but remaining within the Ottoman Empire. The CUP replied with a policy of increasing the centrali-zation of all authority in Istanbul.

In 1911, a completely secret society called Al Fatat – the Young Arab Society – was founded by a group of students in Paris and then transferred to Beirut and Damascus. Its members were sworn to work for complete independence – a step beyond the decentraliza-tion party. In 1914, a secret society was founded among Arab officers in the Turkish army, of whom there were a considerable number, especially Iraqis. The society was called Al Ahad – the Contract or the Covenant. The founder was Aziz al Masri, a major on the Staff of the Turkish Army. It is interesting to note that Aziz al Masri had been a member of the CUP and had taken part in the military revolt which had led to the fall of Sultan Abdul Hamid in 1908. Dissatisfied with the part allotted to the Arabs by the CUP, he started a secret society of army officers to do to the CUP what the CUP had done to the sultan. The idea of secret political societies of young army officers thereby passed on from the Turks to the Arabs.

Thus at the commencement of the First World War, political opinion in Syria and Palestine had been alienated from the CUP – or the 'Young Turks' as they were often called – by the racial discrimination which the government practised in favour of Turks. But we must not visualize the Arab provinces as seething with nationalism. Arab political activity was limited to a very small group of intellectuals, most of them educated in Istanbul and whose very existence was unknown to the great majority of their countrymen.

The ordinary Arabs, eighty per cent of whom could not read or write, had never heard of nationalism and thought of the Ottoman Empire as 'the government' – the only government they could visualize. Outside the towns, they were ever ready to shoot at policemen or soldiers (most of whom were also Arabs), not for nationalist or even for political reasons, but because such people came to collect taxes, to make arrests or – worse still – to take young men away as conscripts for the army.

The governorship of Mecca had been held by the descendants of the Prophet Muhammad, with only a few breaks, ever since the seventh century. The Ottoman Empire had acquired the suzerainty over the Holy Cities when it conquered the Mamelukes in 1517. Since then, the Sublime Porte had maintained the privileges of the Sharifs,[9] the descendants of Muhammad, in Mecca, but had endeavoured to retain their loyalty by removing those who showed too much independence and by promoting the more amenable. On this principle, Abdul Hamid had, in 1892, 'invited' a certain Sharif

Husain ibn Ali to come and live in Istanbul, with his sons Ali, Abdulla and Feisal. Sharif Husain was treated with respect – not to say veneration – and was made a member of the Council of State. He was also kept under observation.

In 1908, the Young Turks, perhaps on the principle of removing all the persons whom Abdul Hamid had appointed and appointing those whom he had removed, dismissed the Grand Sharif of Mecca and sent Sharif Husain to replace him. Husain's second son, Sharif Abdulla, was made member for the Hejaz in the new parliament in Istanbul. In February 1914, Abdulla, returning to Istanbul from Mecca, called on Lord Kitchener in Cairo to sound him regarding Britain's attitude to an Arab revolt against Turkey. Kitchener was cautiously discouraging.

Six months after this interview, the First World War broke out. When Turkey entered the war as the ally of Germany, Britain's position in Egypt and India was threatened, especially as, in November 1914, the sultan declared a Holy War, and appealed to all the Muslims in the world. The contacts established earlier between Lord Kitchener and Sharif Abdulla were renewed and, on 5 June 1916 Sharif Husain led the Arabs of the Hejaz into revolt against the Turks.

A British army was already advancing slowly from Egypt across Sinai to invade Palestine. In January 1917, it was agreed between the Arabs and the British that an Arab army, commanded by Sharif Husain's third son, Feisal, should move northwards and cooperate with the British army on their right flank. On 6 July 1917 an Arab tribal force, accompanied by T. E. Lawrence, captured Aqaba.

On 6 November 1917 the British army under General Allenby had defeated the Turks at Gaza and, on 9 December 1917, Jeru-salem surrendered. The Arabs meanwhile attacked Maan, took Tafila and cut the railway in many places, thereby isolating from Damascus the Turkish garrisons in Medina and Maan.

On 19 September 1918 Allenby completely defeated the Turkish army on a line extending from north of Jaffa to north of Jerusalem.

Two days before, on 17 September, the Arabs had seized Deraa and destroyed the railway which supplied the Turkish army, at the same time cutting off their line of retreat northwards. Damascus was occupied amid scenes of delirious joy and, on 26 October 1918, the allies took Aleppo. On 31 October 1918 Turkey signed an armistice.

The greater part of Syria and Palestine had been behind the Turkish lines throughout the war and had been unable to join in the fighting. Nevertheless the Arab rising in the Hejaz had added fuel to the flames of resentment against Turkey. Jamal Pasha the Less, the governor of Syria, suppressed every attempt at sedition and a number of Arab nationalist leaders were hanged.

The rising in the Hejaz, however, and the operations of the Arabs under Feisal and Lawrence rendered considerable assistance to the British army in Palestine. It has been estimated that they occupied some thirty thousand Turkish troops who would otherwise have been free to fight the British army. In addition, the revolt of Sharif Husain, a descendant of the Prophet Muhammad, rendered ineffective the sultan's appeal for all Muslims to fight against the allies.

The Arab rising in the Hejaz had been preceded by an exchange of letters between Sharif Husain and Sir Henry MacMahon, British High Commissioner in Egypt. In return for this cooperation, the Sharif had asked for a pledge of independence for the whole of the area now included in the peninsula of Arabia, Palestine, Jordan, Lebanon, Syria and Iraq. The British High Commissioner had in general agreed, excluding only an area west of Damascus, Homs, Hama and Aleppo. The correspondence, however, was so loosely worded as to be capable of many interpretations. 'West of Damascus', if Damascus be taken to be the city, presumably meant Lebanon. One of the letters, however, referred to the Province of Damascus, which included all Trans-Jordan down to Aqaba. Thus west of the Province of Damascus would exclude Palestine also. The Husain-MacMahon correspondence never terminated in a formal agreement. It was overtaken by events. The Arab rising broke out, fighting began and the correspondence was dropped.

On 2 November 1917, however, the British government issued the Balfour Declaration, in which it stated that 'His Majesty's Government viewed with favour the establishment in Palestine of a national home for the Jewish people'. Volumes have been written on the ensuing struggle in Palestine, which, however, cannot be treated in this book.

An equally equivocal instrument was the so-called Sykes-Picot Agreement concluded, in May 1916, between France and Britain, in which the two governments agreed to establish zones of influence in the Arab state which was to be set up after the war. In the northern area, which ultimately constituted the present state of Syria, France was to have the priority in local enterprises and the supply of advisers, while in the areas which subsequently became Trans-Jordan and Iraq, Britain was to enjoy that privilege.

In planning this arrangement, Britain may have had in mind a somewhat similar agreement which she had concluded with Russia in 1907. Under this pact, northern Persia was to be open to Russian economic enterprises, while a small area in the south of the country was to be free for British activities. Both the contracting parties promised to respect 'The strict independence and integrity of Persia'. Whereas it is possible that Britain envisaged a similar arrangement in the proposed Arab kingdom, events were to show that France interpreted the plan as direct French rule over Syria.

On the very day of the capture of Damascus by the British and the Arabs, the latter set up their own government. With the full support of the British army, Feisal was made a *de facto* constitutional king. The British had suddenly become aware of the existence of strong nationalist sentiment in Syria, of which they had not realized the intensity during the war, when Syria was still behind the Turkish lines and it was impossible to contact its leaders.

It will be remembered that Syrian nationalism before the First World War was limited to two small secret societies, of the very existence of which the vast majority of Syrians themselves were unaware. It would thus appear that the nationalist feeling had grown during the war, fostered by reports of the revolt in the Hejaz and by the propaganda and promises of the Allies. The Turks themselves had probably contributed much to its intensification through the severe repressive measures adopted by Jamal Pasha the Less in Damascus. Friction had been yet further increased by the charges of treachery freely directed by the Turks against the Arabs. The unexpectedness of this sudden outburst of nationalist fervour in 1918 goes far to explain, if not to justify, the casual political promises made by the Allies during the war. They may not have realized that deep emotions were involved.

In July 1919, the so-called General Syrian Congress assembled in Damascus, claiming to represent Syria, Lebanon, Palestine and Trans-Jordan. It passed a number of resolutions, of which the following is a summary:

(a) Syria, including Palestine, should be recognized as a sovereign state with the Emir Feisal as king.
(b) The Sykes-Picot Agreement and the Balfour Declaration should be repudiated.
(c) Political tutelage should be rejected but foreign assistance should be accepted, if possible from the USA and, if not, from Britain.
(d) French aid in any form was not acceptable.

In September 1919, two Americans, Dr King and Mr Crane, presented a report to President Woodrow Wilson. Their recommendations in brief were as follows:

1 That a mandatory power was necessary but that the mandate should be administered in the interests of Syria alone.
2 That the unity of Syria, Lebanon, Palestine and Trans-Jordan should be respected.
3 That the whole of this area should be under one mandatory, not two.
4 That the United States be the mandatory for the whole area or, failing her, Britain.

Meanwhile the French army had already occupied Lebanon. On 20 July 1920 General Gouraud's army marched on Damascus, which was occupied on 25 July. The Amir Feisal escaped and the Arab state ceased to exist. Britain protested vigorously at the Peace

Conference in Versailles but the French refused to withdraw. Intense resentment was produced between Britain and France and between France and the Syrians.

Arabs have at times accused Britain of having conspired with France to deny independence to Syria in 1920 and to instal direct French rule. Lamentable as was the confusion caused by British diplomatic promises in the First World War, connivance at direct French administration in Syria was not a case in point. The British protests were genuine and still have their repercussions today in 1967.

The whole blame for the confused promises made to the Arabs and to the Jews in 1916 and 1917 has normally been laid on Great Britain. In fact, however, Britain, France and the United States had on several occasions made specific declarations of their intention to ensure the 'complete liberation of the peoples who have for so long been oppressed by the Turks'. France had subscribed to these declarations but, after the war, she seized Syria. The liberation of the peoples subject to the Ottoman Empire had been specifically mentioned in President Woodrow Wilson's fourteen points, yet the United States for the ensuing forty years was to be the strongest supporter of Zionism.

It would, however, be entirely erroneous to attribute to the peoples of these countries any intention of deceiving. Some of the politicians involved were not always straightforward, but perhaps the major part of the blame may be attributed to the very nature of democratic government. The political systems now in vogue in Western nations have three serious drawbacks in so far as foreign affairs are concerned.

Firstly, a considerable degree of inefficiency, foreign affairs being one of several portfolios passed from one politician to another, many of them with no previous experience of the subject.

Secondly, frequent changes of the party in power tend to weaken the determination of politicians to stand by national obligations which had often been assumed by their political rivals.

Thirdly, the development of the system of 'pressure groups', under which small, determined groups of persons are able to exert powerful pressure on governments and politicians, outside parliament or congress, and thereby to change the policy of the nation.

In the bitterness of political recrimination, the very real services rendered by the British and French administrations between the wars have been forgotten. It is difficult for persons who have never lived in these countries to appreciate their predicament in 1920. They had been ruled by the Ottomans for four hundred years, during which the Arabs had no political institutions, no statesmen and no opportunity to gain political experience.

The administrative situation, however, was even worse. Every senior officer or official in the army or the police, in the treasury, the revenue, education, public works and other departments had been an Ottoman Turk. At the end of the war, all these officials departed. The whole administration had to be built up anew and the necessary staff trained to control it. It will be remembered that both the General Syrian Congress and the King-Crane report admitted the need of foreign advice and assistance.

In the twenty years which elapsed between the two wars, an immense amount of devoted work was put into this task by dedicated British officials, who had no connection with politics. The French in Syria were more arbitrary than were the British in Jordan or Iraq, but many French officials were likewise devoted to their administrative work. In the heat of political recrimination, the work of these humbler drones has been forgotten. Nevertheless the fact that after the Second World War these countries were able to administer themselves must be largely attributed to the previous patient labours of these nameless advisers.

The Druzes, as we have seen, are a minority religious group, originally formed in Lebanon. Many of them, however, had migrated after 1861 to a mountainous area south-southeast of Damascus, now known as Jebel al-Druze. On 20 July 1925 the Druzes rose in rebellion against the French. They received little support from the remainder of Syria. Fighting, however, continued until the summer of 1926.

The years from 1930 to 1939 passed uneasily in Syria. Political opposition to the French administration remained unabated but, except for periodical strikes or street demonstrations, there was no further fighting. On 19 September 1936 a treaty between France and Syria was initialled, but was never ratified by the French government. In the interval, the Sanjaq or province of Alexandretta had been ceded to Turkey, much to the indignation of the Syrians. At the outbreak of the Second World War, Syria was still under direct French administration.

Lebanon, like Syria, remained under French rule between the two world wars, but with far less resulting friction. The Lebanese, as we have seen, had looked across the Mediterranean towards the west for several thousand years. Whereas, however, the more enterprising of the Phoenicians had emigrated to North Africa or Spain, the Lebanese of today travel on business to North and South America.

The first Western educational establishments, as early as the sixteenth century, had been opened by French-speaking Jesuits and in the years between the two wars many Lebanese received their education at French institutions in Lebanon or at universities in France. Indeed the visitor to Beirut often found it difficult to distinguish between the French-speaking Lebanese and the French from France. Between peoples so closely related in culture and language, little friction was produced, at least in comparison with the struggles with the Muslim Arabs of Syria.

In the settlement at the end of the First World War, France had assumed direct control of Lebanon and Britain of Palestine. All territory east of Lebanon and of the River Jordan was, according to the British plan, to be an independent Arab state. When, however, the French, in July 1920, occupied Syria, the area east of the River Jordan and south of the Sykes-Picot line, remained without a government, the British having no desire to increase their commitments.

In January 1921, however, the Amir Abdulla, the second son of King Husain,[10] appeared unexpectedly with a force of tribesmen. In March 1921, he occupied Amman unopposed and assumed control, at the same time announcing his intention of driving the French out of Syria. The British were alarmed at the prospect of a war between their two allies. Mr (later Sir) Winston Churchill

came to Jerusalem where he met the Amir Abdulla and an agree/
ment was reached. The Amir was recognized as the ruler of the
territory to which the name of Trans-Jordan was given.

The new state was fortunate in being extremely poor. If occupied
by a foreign power, it was obvious that it would prove a liability
rather than an asset. At the same time, if left without any govern/
ment, it might be made a base for tribal raids into Syria or Palestine.
The Amir Abdulla, as already explained, had been brought up in
Constantinople and had been a member of the Turkish parliament
after the fall of Abdul Hamid. But he had also lived in Mecca and
was familiar with the life of the tribes of Arabia. He was thus able
to deal with the French, the British or the educated Arabs on the one
hand and with the tribes who lived in his new state on the other. As
has already been explained, the people of Syria and Trans-Jordan
consisted of three social groups, the town dwellers, the fellaheen or
cultivators, and the nomads. The three groups felt little sympathy for
one another. The Amir Abdulla possessed the rare qualification of
being able to see the viewpoints of all three.

A British Resident was established in Jordan but the internal
administration was left to the amir and his government. Two
British officers were engaged to train the army and the police, a
British adviser was placed in the Ministry of Justice and another in
that of Finance. As Trans-Jordan was regarded by British officials
as a backwater, the officers who agreed to serve there did so because
they liked the country and the people, not in order to further their
own careers.

As a consequence of these fortunate circumstances, Trans-Jordan
alone, of all the mandated Arab territories, enjoyed peace, progress
and harmony from 1921 to 1939. The stability of the country was
threatened in the period from 1936 to 1939, during which the Arabs
of Palestine were in rebellion, in protest against the massive immi/
gration of Jews. The rebels made strenuous efforts to involve Trans/
Jordan in the disturbances. While, however, many Trans-Jordanians
crossed to Palestine to join in the fighting, they refused to rebel
against their own government – a sure testimonial to the success
achieved by the amir's administration.

The Ottomans, as we have seen, had never been able really to establish control east of the Jordan. In the eighteen years from 1921 to 1939, however, a high standard of public security had been established, roads had been built, schools opened, agricultural machinery imported and the deep loyalty of the people had been won.

Somewhat ironically, Trans-Jordan, a state born out of due time, which nobody wanted and on which no thought, care or negotiations had been expended, was the only really successful mandate which resulted from the First World War.

KEY DATES

1876–1909	Reign of the Ottoman Sultan Abdul Hamid
1908	Ottoman army *coup d'état*
1909	Abdul Hamid deposed. The Committee of Union and Progress assume power
May 1916	Signature of the secret Sykes-Picot agreement
June 1916	Revolt of Sharif Husain of Mecca (later to be called King Husain of the Hejaz)
November 1917	Publication of the Balfour Declaration
25 July 1920	French occupation of Damascus
1925–6	Druze Rebellion in Syria
1936–9	Arab rebellion in Palestine

17 The city of Jerusalem is holy to Jews, Christians and Muslims alike. Part of the alignment of the present walls dates from King Solomon. The walls shown here were rebuilt by the Ottomans on the foundations of Herod's Wall.

18 Christ often walked along the road from Jerusalem to Jericho seen in this photograph. It was here that He laid the scene of the parable of the Good Samaritan. This track was famous for highway robbers even in the present century.

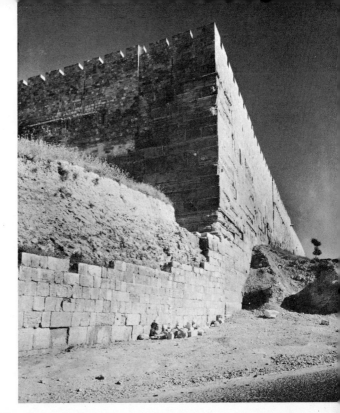

9 (*left*) The Mount of Olives, the scene
of the Ascension. The churches in the
centre mark the site of the Garden of
Gethsemane.

10 (*below left*) Jerusalem seen from the air
showing the Arab portion of the city. In
the centre is the Dome of the Rock and the
walls of the old city.

11 (*right*) The Dome of the Rock,
erroneously called the Mosque of Omar, was
built by the Caliph Abdul Malik in AD 688.
The oldest surviving monument of Muslim
architecture, it was originally faced with
marble and polychrome mosaic. The present
glazed tiles were substituted in 1552 by the
Sultan Sulaiman the Magnificent.

12 (*below*) This large mass of naked rock
under the Dome is alleged to have been the
place where Abraham prepared to sacrifice
Isaac. Until AD 135 it was used by the
Jews for sacrifices. Muslims believe that
Muhammad started from it on his nocturnal
journey to Heaven.

23 (*left*) As the result of an appeal by Pope Urban II in 1095, the First Crusade was launched. Crac des Chevaliers was the most famous of the great castles used to defend the crusader states.

24 (*below left*) The Seventh Crusade was commanded by Saint Louis IX, King of France in 1249. This page from a mediaeval manuscript shows the capture of Damietta by Louis.

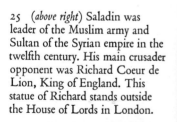

25 (*above right*) Saladin was leader of the Muslim army and Sultan of the Syrian empire in the twelfth century. His main crusader opponent was Richard Coeur de Lion, King of England. This statue of Richard stands outside the House of Lords in London.

26 (*right*) The tomb of Saladin in Damascus near the famous Ummayad mosque was restored by Kaiser Wilhelm II of Germany in 1893.

27   Syro-Palestine was part of the Ottoman empire for 400 years. One of its most prominent rulers was Sultan Abdul Hamid II, who ruled from 1876 until his deposition in 1909 by the revolutionary Committee of Union and Progress.

28   Sharif Husain's third son, Feisal, led the desert army (seen here) which assisted the British forces in defeating the Turks in the First World War.

29 The Hejaz railway from Damascus to Medina built by Abdul Hamid II was used for the transportation of Turkish prisoners. It was this railway which was frequently blown up by T. E. Lawrence.

30 General Chauvel at the head of the British cavalry entering Damascus in September 1918. A month later, Turkey asked for an armistice.

31 The British army took Jerusalem on 9 December 1917. The Commander-in-Chief, General Allenby, modestly made his entry into the Holy City on foot.

32 The Jordan army, formerly known as the Arab Legion, was originally mounted on thorough-bred Arab horses. It is now completely mechanized.

9   Unity or diversity :
1939-1966

At the outbreak of the Second World War, Syro-Palestine politics were agitated by two major grievances – the continuance of direct French administration in Syria and Lebanon, and the influx of Jewish immigrants into Palestine. At the end of the First World War, Britain had been looked upon as the friend of the Arabs. Her opposition to direct French administration in Syria, her abandonment of the mandate over Iraq in 1932 and the successful progress achieved in Trans-Jordan had created the impression that she was the most reasonable and sympathetic of the Great Powers. From 1936 onwards, however, the increased Jewish immigration into Palestine and the resulting Arab rebellion reversed this situation and rendered Britain perhaps even more unpopular than France.

According to allied stategic plans at the beginning of the Second World War, France was to be responsible for the defence of Syria and the neighbouring states, while Britain was to concentrate on the defence of Egypt. A large French army was built up for this purpose in Syria and Lebanon under the command of General Weygand. There were no British ground troops in Iraq or Trans-Jordan, and most of those in Palestine were moved to Egypt.

With the fall of France in the summer of 1940, an Italo-German Armistice Commission assumed control in Syria. The large French army on which Britain had relied for the defence of the Middle

East assumed an attitude of hostile inactivity. In March 1941, an Italo-German offensive developed in the Western Desert of Egypt. In April, a pro-German military *coup d'état* took place in Iraq and the new government declared war on Britain, who was now fighting alone in the world.

In this situation Syria remained quiet, the French army in the country being amply strong to keep order. In general, Syrian politicians probably hoped for a German victory. In Palestine Jews and Arabs alike proclaimed a truce in their struggles and professed support for Britain, though without any great enthusiasm.

In Trans-Jordan, the only country where the mandatory system had worked successfully, the Amir Abdulla actually declared war on Germany, at a moment when the whole world was convinced of the imminence of a German victory. In pursuance of this policy, the Jordan Army (The Arab Legion) accompanied a small British column from Palestine which crossed the desert and overthrew the pro-German régime in Baghdad. 'Britain has helped Trans-Jordan', said the Amir Abdulla, 'and Arabs do not abandon their friends just because they are in trouble.'

On 8 June 1941 the British army, accompanied by a column of Free French and an Arab Legion Force, crossed the frontier into Syria. After nineteen days of fighting against the Vichy government French, Syria was occupied and handed over to the Free French or Gaullists to continue the administration during the war.

The invasion of Syria had been preceded by some intensive political activity. It will be remembered that in the First World War, Britain had promised independence to Syria, but that the French army had occupied the country and had refused to honour the promise. The incident had rankled and when the Second World War produced a similar situation, the British government were determined to avoid a repetition of broken promises. In return for British agreement to hand over Syria and Lebanon to Free French administration during the period of the war, General Catroux, representing General de Gaulle, announced in a broadcast to Syria from Egypt, 'I come to put an end to the mandatory régime and to proclaim you free and independent.'

For two years after the occupation of Syria, the pledge went unfulfilled owing to the precarious military situation. At the end of 1943, negotiations commenced between the Free French and the Syrian and Lebanese governments but little progress was achieved. After the war, in May 1945, negotiations were resumed when suddenly French military reinforcements landed in Beirut. The Syrians thereupon broke off negotiations and on 30 May 1945, street fighting broke out in Damascus, Homs, Hama and Aleppo. Thereupon the British government ordered British troops to take over public security duties in Syria and French troops were requested to return to their barracks. Early in 1946, British and French troops alike withdrew from Syria and Lebanon. Thirty years after the exchange of letters between Sir Henry MacMahon and Sharif Husain, Syria achieved her independence.

At the end of the Second World War, Britain seemed to be every, where supreme in the Middle East. Her armies were in occupation of Persia, Iraq, Syria, Lebanon, Palestine and Egypt. The victorious conclusion of the war, after the dark years 1940–1 in which Britain had faced the world alone, could not fail to enhance her prestige, while her forcible intervention to secure the independence of Syria had earned the enthusiastic gratitude of the people of that country.

On 22 March 1945 the Charter of the Arab League was signed in Cairo. In spite of accusations still occasionally heard that Britain has tried to prevent the Arab states from uniting, the British govern, ment used all its influence to assist in the formation of the Arab League. The foundation members were Egypt, Syria, Lebanon, Jordan, Iraq, Saudi Arabia and the Yemen. The Arab League gave birth to an entirely new development, namely Egyptian align, ment with the cause of Arab nationalism. Prior to 1945, the loyalty of Egyptians had been to Egypt alone and Syria had been the original champion of Arabism. Now Egypt aspired to take the lead. At the end of the Second World War, Britain was extremely anxious to retain Arab friendship, though she no longer had any desire to rule them. Before, however, a permanent amicable settlement could be achieved, two problems, both inherited from a former generation, remained to be cleared up. They were the Arab-Jewish rivalry in Palestine and relations between Britain and Egypt.

The Palestine problem was the first to explode. Violent passions made themselves felt even before the Second World War was over. Jewish terrorist organizations in Palestine denounced Britain as their principal enemy, although it was she who had in fact made Zionist settlement in Palestine possible. The Arabs, on the other hand, accused Britain of conspiring with the Zionist to render Arab unity impossible. At the same time the United States, emerging from the Second World War with immensely enhanced prestige, threw her weight on the side of the Jews. Denounced by so many conflicting powers, Britain resigned her mandate and gave notice to the United Nations that she would withdraw her forces on 15 May 1948. The mandate had originally been allotted by the League of Nations, of which the United Nations Organization was assumed to be the heir.

The idea of dividing Palestine into Jewish and Arab sections had first been proposed by the Peel Commission, sent out to investigate the situation during the Arab rebellion of 1936–9. The idea was now revived by UNO and a new partition plan, considerably modified in favour of the Jews, was produced by an international commission. The Arab governments unwisely decided to boycott the debate in the United Nations General Assembly, with the result that the proposal was accepted, though only after a great deal of lobbying.

The plan was by no means easy to implement, owing to the presence of as many Arabs as there were Jews in the areas allotted to the Jewish state. If, however, Britain or the United Nations had provided sufficient armed forces to keep the peace, some exchanges of population and payments of compensation might have facilitated the process. No such forces were provided.

The Arab states had unwisely, in their attempts to support the Arabs of Palestine, made use of threats of force, without having seriously prepared for action. Suffice it to say that the Egyptian army invaded southern Palestine. Lebanon had virtually no army and was unable to take any effective military action. The Syrian army went into action south of the Sea of Galilee but was repulsed. A small contingent was sent five hundred miles across the desert from Iraq. Anguished appeals to the Jordan government from the Arab population of Palestine resulted in the despatch of the Jordan army (The Arab Legion) to defend the Arab areas of Palestine.

In February, March and April 1949, armistices were signed in Rhodes between various Arab governments and the newly estab-lished government of Israel. Samaria and Judaea were subsequently united to the Kingdom of Jordan. Thenceforward the old Syro-Palestine country was divided into four independent states – Lebanon, Syria, Jordan and Israel. Britain, the friend of the Arabs at the end of the Second World War, was everywhere execrated and detested as the engineer of the state of Israel. (See map VII, pages 210–11.)

From 1950 onwards, the various political pressures which have been brought to bear on Syria, Lebanon and Jordan may be listed under a number of heads.

1 One of the strongest sentiments among educated Syrians was the hope of Arab unity, founded on two main considerations. The first of these was the memory of the past glories of Syria and the Arab Empire. The second was the more negative feeling of resentment at the domination of the Great Powers, Turkey, Britain, France, the United States and Russia. The existing Arab states, it was felt, were too small. Only by the union of all the Arab countries would they be able to constitute a nation strong enough to stand up to the Great Powers.

The Arabic-speaking peoples, however, are emotional, excitable and impatient. When a political objective is adopted, its adherents look for immediate action, without allowing time for the preparation of the details. The result has been several false starts, proclamations of Arab unity which have subsequently been found impossible to implement.

The most dramatic of these attempts was the announcement of the union of Syria and Egypt on 22 February 1958, under the name of the United Arab Republic. Propaganda to the effect that all

145

Arabic-speaking peoples were one nation had obscured the fact that the Egyptians and the Syrians are in reality two very different races. The Syrians are extremely quick-witted, unstable and impatient of authority. The Egyptians, on the other hand, are orderly, submissive and comparatively easy to rule.

'You will find Syria a difficult country to govern,' Shukri al Kuwatly, the Syrian President, is alleged to have told Jamal Abdul Nasser, the Egyptian President. 'Fifty per cent of the Syrians consider themselves national leaders, twenty-five per cent think they are prophets and ten per cent imagine they are gods.'[11]

The difference in temperament between the two peoples soon made itself felt and, in September 1961, the union was terminated.

2 A second problem which has confronted Syria, Lebanon and Jordan since the Second World War has been that of discovering a form of government suitable to Arab peoples and yet at the same time adapted to the modern world.

At all periods of history, the customs, culture, dress and institutions of the leading powers of the time have been sedulously imitated by weaker nations. During the centuries of Arab Empire, the west European nations enthusiastically copied the Arabs.

After the First World War, British or American democracy was looked upon by many thoughtful Arabs as the model to be imitated. The unpopularity of the Western Democracies since the Second World War has caused a number of Arabs to look with favour upon Soviet Russia. In all such cases equally, however, the origin of the system advocated was imitation of some other nation.

In Egypt President Nasser, and in Syria the Baath or Renaissance Party, adopted the name of Arab socialism. The social organization of the Egyptian people is, however, as a result of many centuries of past history, entirely different from that of Syria. Vague political aspirations, making use of foreign party labels, are not in themselves of much value.

3 Even in the days of King Faruk, Egyptian aspirations to dominate the Arab League, if not to rule an Arab Empire, introduced a further complication. When President Nasser assumed control, he owed much of his immense popularity in the Arab world to the

belief that he was about to destroy the state of Israel. So intense was the enthusiasm evoked that it appeared for a few heady years that he might unite many Arab countries into a real empire.

When, however, the years rolled by and Israel remained uncon-quered, the Egyptian régime was obliged to seek other activities in order to maintain the initiative. The result was a programme of socialism and nationalization, the enforcement of which did much to cause the breakdown of the union with Syria.

While the Egyptian version of Arab socialism could claim credit for a number of internal reforms, President Nasser employed it also as a weapon of attack against those Arab rulers who were unwilling to accept his leadership. The announcement that socialism alone could bring prosperity and progress to the Arabs enabled him to denounce as reactionaries all monarchies, and even republics, whose ideologies were not identical with his own. The Nasser régime developed a violently worded propaganda, particularly in their broadcasting, in which Egypt was represented in every Arab country as the friend of the people, who were being oppressed and exploited by their 'reactionary' rulers.

Syrian political leaders may be divided, by and large, into two groups – intellectuals who were political theorists and army officers who were more practical but perhaps more arbitrary. As has already been noted, many Syrian army officers are in fact drawn from the same class of intellectuals as the politicians, but even a short period of army service somewhat modifies their outlook.

Each of these two classes was to some extent a reaction from the other. The theorists often proved incapable when faced with the actual task of government. The soldiers were exposed to the criticisms of the intellectuals for their arbitrary actions. The soldiers, however, it is to be noted, were not conservative, as in so many Western countries. On the contrary, they had inherited from Otto-man days and through President Nasser the tradition of the revolu-tionary young officer. The result of these stresses was an apparently endless succession of *coups d'état*.

This instability provided many opportunities for interference and intrigue, primarily by the Nasser régime but at times also by Iraq.

147

Once again we are reminded of the dawn of history and of Syria as the cockpit between the Pharaohs and the Assyrians.

We have seen how often in history Lebanon looked for an exchange of ideas and for her commercial prosperity, not to the Arab hinterland but to the Mediterranean and the West. It is, therefore, of interest to note that she is the only Arabic-speaking country in the Middle East which has successfully operated a comparatively free and democratic constitution since 1946. For such systems of govern-ment are not indigenous to the Arab countries but are the product of Western thought and temperament.

It is true that in July 1958, at the height of President Nasser's expansionist period, a somewhat half-hearted revolution broke out in Lebanon. United States troops were landed and remained for some weeks until order was restored. There was in fact virtually no fighting in connection with this episode.

Since 1958, Lebanese politics have proceeded without major incident. The fact that Lebanon has always been a refuge for minority sects may have produced in the Lebanese a spirit of mutual toleration. Moreover, a high proportion of Lebanese study abroad or in foreign institutions at home, like the American University of Beirut or the Roman Catholic Université de Saint Joseph. An even greater proportion travel or settle abroad for business purposes, in the countries round the Mediterranean or in North or South America. A considerable part of the revenue of Lebanon takes the form of remittances from abroad.

More emotional Arab nationalists from neighbouring countries tend to disparage the Lebanese as being too engrossed in money making to sacrifice themselves for the cause of Arab racialism, but the result has certainly produced a more stable political atmosphere than in Syria. Lebanon has also achieved some prosperity as a tourist country, largely patronized by Iraqis, Syrians, Saudis and Egyptians. Here, in the mountain resorts, relief can be obtained from the summer heats of other Arab countries, while patrons who feel so inclined can also enjoy the slightly meretricious gaieties of a pseudo-French riviera.

In contrast with the international frivolities of Beirut, Jordan offers a more purely Arabian atmosphere. The Lebanese, as we have seen, are ethnically of extremely mixed descent, from the earliest invaders such as the Hittites, through Greeks, Italians and Ottomans to modern French.

Jordan, east of the river of that name, is contiguous with the Syrian desert and on the south with central Arabia and the Hejaz. Thus the largest ingredient in the Jordanian racial mixture is probably old Arabian from the desert. Town populations, as in all Arab countries, are doubtless slightly more mixed – the ten Greek cities founded after Alexander lay largely in Jordan, and their populations have doubtless disappeared into the people of the towns north of Amman. There are also a few Circassian towns and villages, inhabited by immigrants who have arrived within the last hundred years.

About eight per cent of the inhabitants of Jordan are Christians, many of them resident in Jerusalem or Amman. The towns of Bethlehem, Ramallah, Madeba, famous for the Byzantine mosaic on the floor of its church, and Al Husn, near Irbid, are almost entirely Christian. East of the Dead Sea, the picturesque town of Kerak was for some seventy-five years a famous Crusader fortress. There are still one or two small tribes outside the town called by such names as the 'Franks', and the 'Parishioners'. Curiously enough these small groups are now Muslims.

There is, however, a strong Christian element in Kerak. More or less isolated for centuries from the outside world, the Muslims and Christians grew near to one another. Puzzled, perhaps, at the existence of two creeds in so small a community, some people seem to have endeavoured to make sure of salvation by belonging simul-taneously to both. An ancient building in the town was used alternately for prayers by Muslims and Christians. Only in compara-tively recent years have the two communities become quite distinct, partly as a result of the activities of European Christian missionaries.

In general, however, Jordan is fortunate in the homogeneity of its inhabitants, the great majority of whom are Sunni Muslims, largely of Arabian descent. An exception must, however, be made in the

149

case of the refugees from Palestine who fled from the coastal plain in 1948.

The towns of the coastal plain, as already noted, were at one time inhabited by the Philistines, probably an immigrant race from Greece. In Seleucid times, the area, like Lebanon, was largely Hellenized. In New Testament times, the Roman headquarters was at Caesarea, twenty-four miles south of Haifa, and not in Jerusalem. For two centuries, the coastal plain was held by the Crusaders, some portion of whose blood must have become intermingled with that of the indigenous peoples. As a result, the Palestine refugees, who now constitute about one-third of the people of Jordan, are doubtless of more mixed origin than the original inhabitants of the area east of the river.

On 24 April 1950 the union with Trans-Jordan of that part of Palestine which was still held by the Arabs, was officially announced in Amman. The new state was called the Kingdom of Jordan. Since then, the population of Jordan has consisted of three different groups, each representing about one-third of the total. The original people of Trans-Jordan, overwhelmingly Arab in their ethnic origin, constitute the first third. The second third consists of the refugees, the former residents of the coastal plain, of partly Semitic and partly European origin. The third group is composed of the inhabitants of the hill country of Palestine, still resident in their homes in Judaea and Samaria, and whose ethnic origin is intermediate between that of the former coast dwellers and those east of the Jordan.

The town dwellers of Jerusalem and Nablus, the only two large Arab towns remaining west of the Jordan, are, as usual, considerably more mixed with foreign blood than are the villagers, who differ only in a slight degree from the villagers in the mountains east of the Jordan.

Ideally, the brilliantly intellectual gifts of the coast dwellers – now the refugees – should combine perfectly with the more stolid and virile Arabs of the east to form a balanced community. Unfortunately, however, the different mentalities of these two ethnic groups tend to produce animosity rather than cooperation.

The principal problem confronting Jordan today is how to combine the populations east and west of the Jordan into a harmonious
whole. The friction periodically visible between the two sections is
commonly imputed to political differences. In reality, however,
deeper differences of ethnic origin probably account for part of the
problem.

As already indicated, Anglo-Jordan relations in the period from
1921 to 1948 were exceptionally happy. The establishment of the
state of Israel in 1948, however, the resultant fighting and the influx
of some half a million embittered refugees somewhat impaired this
harmony. In July 1951, King Abdulla, who had founded Trans-
Jordan in 1921 and had ruled it patriarchally for thirty years, was
assassinated in Jerusalem. Friction increased in the years 1954–6, as
a result of the rapid rise of Nasserism in Egypt. At this time,
President Nasser was looked upon as the Arab champion against
Israel, a role which made a strong appeal to Palestinian Arabs,
especially the refugees.

In 1955, Anglo-Jordan talks with a view to the adherence of
Jordan to the Baghdad Pact, directed against communism, were
denounced by the Egyptian government as an underhand means of
aiding Israel against the Arabs. The logic of this interpretation was
not immediately obvious but the theme was one calculated to arouse
the deepest emotion, and riots resulted in Jordan. Partly as a result
of further pressure from Egypt, British officers in the Jordan army
were dismissed in April 1956. Later the Anglo-Jordan Treaty was
abrogated, and a state of political instability resulted.

In April 1957, however, a counter-revolution occurred, politically
extremist officers escaped to Egypt or Syria and the king resumed
authority. In 1958, however, the Iraqi revolution, with the assassination of King Feisal II and of the heir apparent, both cousins of
King Husain, once again introduced a period of uncertainty.
British troops were flown in to Jordan, at the same time as the
American forces disembarked at Beirut. A few weeks later, the
situation having settled down, the troops were withdrawn.

Relations with Egypt remained strained, notably from 1961 to
1964, during which time President Nasser was emphasizing his

policy of revolutionary socialism, partly as a weapon to discredit his rivals. In January 1964, however, an Arab 'Summit Conference' was held in Cairo at which Nasser so far tempered his revolutionary enthusiasm as to embrace the two 'reactionaries', King Saud ibn Saud and King Husain of Jordan.

During the years from 1958 to 1966, King Husain steadily improved his position in Jordan. The country regained much of its old reputation for stability, acquired under Husain's grandfather, King Abdulla, in the period from 1921 to 1948. In November 1966, however, following on an Israeli attack on a village south of Hebron, riots broke out once more in Jerusalem, Ramallah and Nablus.

KEY DATES

1936–9	Arab rebellion in Palestine
1940	Control of Syria and Lebanon assumed by Italo-German Commission
1941	Declaration of war by Jordan on Germany
April 1941	Declaration of war by Iraq on Britain after military *coup d'état*
May 1941	Recapture of Baghdad by a British column and The Arab Legion
June 1941	Occupation of Syria by the British army, Free French and The Arab Legion
22 March 1945	Signature of the Arab League Charter
1948	British Evacuation of Palestine
May 1948– March 1949	Arab–Israel hostilities
April 1956	Dismissal of British officers from The Arab Legion
14 March 1957	Termination of the Anglo-Jordan Treaty
22 February 1958	Union of Syria and Egypt
July 1958	Disturbances in the Lebanon. Landing of American troops
September 1961	End of Syro-Egyptian Union

10   The bedouins

A HISTORICAL SKETCH OF SYRIA, Lebanon and Jordan
inevitably consists largely of politics, wars and governments. Yet
these aspects of national affairs give little indication of the way of life
of the people. It has already been explained that the populations of
Syria and Jordan today consist of three communities, the nomads,
the cultivators and the city-dwellers. We will consider each of these
three communities separately.

It has already been seen that, for many thousands of years, the
populations of Syria, Lebanon and Jordan have been recruited from
two entirely distinct sources. From the north and west have come
various races, Indo-European, Turkic, Armenoid and others. From
the south and east have come 'Arabs' from the Arabian peninsula.
Measurement of their skulls shows that dwellers on the coast of the
Mediterranean are today of a different race from those of the desert.

Nomadism was, and still is, necessary to the economy of the Arab
countries. The rains, or the rivers available for irrigation, are so
scarce that all lands sufficiently well watered are used for agriculture
and none can be spared for grazing. During the winter and spring,
however, grass and shrubs grow here and there in the desert.
Breeders of sheep, goats or camels consequently move into the desert
at the beginning of winter. But rain does not fall uniformly over the
desert, even in winter. The first rain is often brought by a violent
thunderstorm which is borne rapidly from the Mediterranean across
the mountains of Lebanon or Palestine and continues eastwards
across the desert to Iraq.

Often in the dry and dusty autumn, when no rain has fallen for seven months, the distant rumble of thunder may be heard or, far away beneath the night horizon, the pale reflections of lightning-flashes in the black sky of night. Then the nomads will gather in front of their tents, trying to estimate where the storm is passing. At dawn, camel riders set out to reconnoitre. For forty or fifty miles, they will ride across the dry, dusty desert hills. Then suddenly the earth will be wet, pools of water lie in the rocky valleys and the earth and air are washed and clean.

The riders turn the heads of their camels, tapping them into a trot with their canes. Great is the rejoicing when they ride once more into the dusty but expectant camp, crying aloud, 'Good news! good news! The wadi[12] al-Hasa has been in flood and is full of pools.'

Early next morning all is noise and bustle. Tents fall and are rolled up and loaded on camels. The men gather round the dying camp-fires for a last cup of coffee before mounting. Then the groaning camels lurch to their feet and the whole convoy is on the move. In front rides the shaikh with a small advanced guard of horse and camel riders, some with hawks on their wrists or greyhounds trotting behind them. A few hundred yards behind come the great camels bearing the swaying litters, hung with tassels and blue beads, from which the black-eyed beauties of the tribe look down upon the world. Boys chase one another, camel riders sing, the world is gay, for the rains have come and in front lie the vast expanses of the desert, range behind range of faint blue hills, space, freedom, grazing and spring.

But in April or May, the sun beats fiercely down once more. The grass has dried and the desert has assumed an even fawn colour, dancing in the mirage. The water pools are empty and the dust-devils, tiny independent cyclones, race across the plains raising twisting corkscrews of dust a hundred feet high. A few of the tougher tribes will spend the whole summer camped on some deep well far out in the desert, but the majority will move slowly back to the fringe of the cultivated area.

Harvest is in May in these sunny climates, after which the nomad flocks are often turned into the stubble – a process to which the

154

farmers are not averse, for the animals manure the land before the autumn ploughing.

Now is the time when the bedouin family must sell their year's produce. Those who have sheep or goats will have wool or oil for sale or young lambs for the meat market. Later perhaps a camel will be sold to complete the supplies needed for the autumn return to the desert. Sacks of flour, rice and dates will be required, a new shirt and perhaps a cloak for each member of the family and, for the well-to-do, a strip of carpet or a coarse quilt. Such are the simple needs of the nomad family.

The black tent of the bedouin is made of long woven strips of goathair, roughly stitched together, and is supported on poles and held up by long ropes attached to tent pegs. It forms a kind of overhead awning, to which curtains are hung along the sides and across the ends, one side being usually left open. The tents vary in size from six or seven feet each way to the great tents of important chiefs which may be twenty or thirty yards long.

The austerities of nomadic life prohibit social classes. The impossibility of transporting furniture obliges all to sit on the ground, thereby effecting a democratic levelling of social barriers. Arab tradition attaches great importance to genealogy with the result that a family of shaikhs or tribal chiefs is treated with respect. But even the greatest nomad chief is only the first among his equals and is rarely, if ever, able to give an order, far less inflict a punishment.

No settled government established in a great capital city like Antioch or Damascus, was ever able to control the bedouin tribes. Such governments maintained armies of cavalry, infantry and artillery to defend their countries but none of these forces could move in the desert, where the camel alone was supreme. As a result, for thousands of years, the tribes behaved like independent nations, declaring war upon one another, making peace or concluding alliances.

But bedouin warfare was distinguished by certain peculiarities, which have left a profound impression on human development. Life in the desert was always precarious. Not only did other human beings present a constant danger, but the forces of nature were allied to destroy mankind. Wolves and hyaenas were constantly at hand, ready to prey on the flocks, which the shepherd boy, often still a child, would be expected to protect.

At any moment, as the result of some careless action, the blind desert itself was ready to claim its victim. Boys in their early teens would become accustomed to crossing hundreds of miles of desert by camel, alternately scanning the horizon for hostile riders, or the tracks in the sand for the passage of raiding parties or dangerous wild animals. If the rider dismounted for a moment and let go the head-rope of his camel, the animal might shy away and disappear over the skyline, leaving him to a lingering death from thirst.

Life under such conditions produced men of strong personality, complete self-reliance and quick decision. But it seems also to have developed a resigned philosophy, for death was always near. The empty vastness of the desert, moreover, inspired in the nomad a sense of God filling the world but the bare simplicity of his own existence bred in him an indifference to hair-splitting dogma or elaborate ritual.

Many of these characteristics, originally the result of the struggle for survival in the desert, were incorporated into the Muslim religion. It has often been stated in the West that Islam, by advocating resignation to God's will, has made its adherents supine and lacking in energy. This estimate is erroneous. The majority of the Arabs of Arabia are extremely active and full of initiative, but when all their efforts have failed, they accept death or disaster without regret as the will of God.

In the old days, bedouin wars happened spontaneously when two tribes collided, but they were not normally entered upon with any definite political objective in view. No one expected tribal wars to end or to be followed by a period of peace. Hostility between men was endemic, like the attacks of beasts of prey or the ravages of disease. The bedouin's object in war, therefore, was not a victorious peace. To some extent it was the survival of his tribe, but to an equal degree it was to gain personal distinction. To become a knightly hero was his aim and the recounting of gallant episodes of war lent glamour and imagination to his otherwise almost unbearably hard existence.

The combination of these two factors – wars with no political object and the deeply marked personalities of men who trusted in their own resourcefulness to survive– produced chivalrous war. The object of the fighter was not to win the war but to perform some startlingly splendid action. As an example, to surprise an enemy encampment at night might bring victory, but to notify the enemy in advance of the time of one's attack would be more honourable and would earn greater glory for the attacker. Even before the appearance of Islam in the seventh century AD, rival tribes often agreed on the place and date of a pitched battle, long before the event.

When a major tribal battle of this kind took place, the rival 'armies' would first draw up opposite one another. Then an interval of time would be allowed for champions. A horseman would ride out from one side, calling out his titles and perhaps the name of a girl. Immediately another would emerge from the opposite party and the two would ride against one another shouting their war cries or the names of ladies. Only when all the champions had satisfied their passion for honour, did the real battle begin.

Often girls rode into battle in gaily decorated camel litters, as a rallying point for their kinsmen. When fighting began, the girls would let down their long hair, bare their breasts, recite poetry or sing the ballads of past tribal heroes. Needless to say such girls were never interfered with by the men of either side. If accidentally captured, they were sent back under escort to their relatives.

It was these same nomadic tribesmen who formed the raw material of the Muslim armies which overran so great a part of the civilized world from the Atlantic to the frontiers of China in the century from AD 632 to 732.

For two or three hundred years, their institutions were imitated and admired from the Pyrenees to the Sahara, and from the Atlantic to Turkestan. The characteristics of their culture may be summarized as, firstly, chivalry in war, that is to say the belief that it is better to lose the battle than to fight dishonourably. Secondly, lavish hospitality and a devotion to poetry. But, thirdly, the root of these customs lay in the deep individual development of the personalities of men who, in a wild country, relied each on himself for survival.

These peculiarities were carried by the conquering Arabs to Spain and southern France. Strength is always admired by men and the peoples of western Europe for several centuries diligently imitated the customs of the Arabs, just as today the peoples of Asia aspire to follow the customs of the West. The result was to produce the chivalry of mediaeval Europe, a copy of bedouin mentality refined, in its later years, by the more tender spirit of Christianity. Shake speare was reproducing a typical bedouin outburst when he made *Henry V*, rejecting the idea of more men at the Battle of Agincourt, cry out:

'But if it be a sin to covet honour,
I am the most offending soul alive.'

In war, the Greeks and the Romans were not romantics. They fought to win and every means used to that end was legitimate. After the Arab conquests in the seventh and eighth centuries, western Europe gradually absorbed the idea of chivalrous war, con ducted with courtesy as a means of gaining honour. But religious prejudice later caused the abandonment of Muslim customs, and a reversion to the example of the Romans. As a result we are now faced with the problem of total war, nuclear warfare, chemical war fare and wholesale genocide. For our sole object is to win, regardless alike of military honour and of Christian charity.

The individualism of the bedouins, however, gave rise to serious complications when these men found themselves collected in cities as the ruling class of a great empire. For every free Arab was a law unto himself with little feeling for the community. Frequent feuds, rebellions and civil wars were the result.

The other outstanding quality of the bedouins is hospitality. In so vast a land without human habitations, not to say hotels, to refuse hospitality to the traveller would often be tantamount to sentencing him to death. But, as in war, the bedouin cannot be content to do just what is necessary. He must do ten times what is necessary and do it with a flourish and a *panache* as well.

The guest, even if a completely unknown stranger, must be greeted with cries of welcome. He must be entertained for three days before it is even legitimate to ask him where he came from or where he is going. Should an enemy arrive in search of him, the host must, if necessary, sacrifice his life to defend his guest from injury. For the bedouin's tent is his castle, where the weak and the oppressed may take refuge. An Arab nomad, living with his family at what we should consider far below the subsistence level, will kill his last sheep to provide a banquet for a complete stranger whom he has never seen before and will never see again. His honour compels him to do so.

The bedouin way of life, however, had many faults. The constant competition between men in their pursuit of honour led to bitter rivalries and jealousy. Originally imitated from the Arabs, they led to constant hostility between the barons of mediaeval Europe, ultimately terminating in the practice of duelling between gentlemen.

The deeply marked individuality of the bedouin and his thirst for personal honour resulted in a neglect of the public interest and an absence of loyalty to the community. And finally, the Arab pride in hospitality and generosity produced an utterly improvident view of life. The heroes of the Arab heroic ballads are invariably brave, courteous to ladies and fantastically hospitable and generous but never rich.

The distinctive culture which they produced exerted a profound influence on human thought for a thousand years but it was the result of the life which they led in the desert, cut off from the remainder of the human race. Only since the 1930s has this situation changed. Whereas the inaccessibility of the desert preserved for thousands of years the marked individuality of the bedouins, the internal combustion engine destroyed their independence in ten years. On their wide rolling plains, the great flocks of the nomads were entirely at the mercy of the machine gun, the armoured car and the aircraft of our time.

At the same time, the discovery of oil and other forms of indus-trialism have opened new ways of life. The immemorial life of the nomad has undergone profound changes, particularly in its moral and imaginative form. Hollywood films – as elsewhere in the world – are destroying the ideals of romantic love, and the urge to earn money is replacing the desire to win honour.

But if the bedouin way of life is in danger of extinction, the hatreds which they aroused when they were to be feared are only gradually weakening. Like most human beings, the bedouins when they were powerful were often arrogant and oppressive. Hatred of their past outrages is deeply engrained in both the villagers and the city-dwellers who were formerly their victims.

It is somewhat ironical that those who today are the most vocal defenders of 'Arabism' are at the same time the most bitter in their scornful denunciations of the nomads. Yet it is difficult to deny that the bedouins in fact represent the real quintessence of Arabism, almost entirely unadulterated by foreign influence. Although they now count for nothing in public life, it was their marked individualism which originally made the Arabs great.

(*above left*) King Abdulla, who ruled Jordan from 1921 to 1951, supported Britain in the Second World War. In 1940, he declared war on Germany on his own initiative.

(*above right*) His grandson King Husain is the present King of Jordan.

(*below left*) Fróm 1939 to 1956, the Commander of the Jordanian army was Glubb Pasha (*centre*) here ꞁ with King Abdulla (*right*).

(*below right*) President Nasser of Egypt with King Husain.

37 (*left*) The Port of Aqaba under construction in 1960; it is Jordan's only port.

38 (*below left*) Local industry caters for the countless Christian pilgrims who come to the Holy Land. Fashioning mother-of-pearl for religious souvenirs at Bethlehem.

39 (*right*) Agriculture is vital to Jordan's economy. Primitive and picturesque methods such as threshing wheat with a sledge have now in many places been supplanted by more modern machinery.

40 (*below*) Breeders of sheep and goats move into the desert at the beginning of winter, when grass and shrubs begin to grow.

41 (*above*) The valleys and mountain slopes of Lebanon provide good soil and climatic conditions for growing fruit, Lebanon's most important agricultural crop. A banana plantation in the valley of Bait al Din in Lebanon.

42 (*below far left*) The wonderful variety of fruits grown in Lebanon is displayed for sale at local stalls. This one is in Beirut.

43 (*below left*) Textiles are produced for export. A beaming machine at a textile factory in Lebanon.

44 (*right*) The courtyard of the Palace Bait al Din in Lebanon. The palace was built for Bashir al Shihabi in the sixteenth century.

45 (*below*) On the shore of the Mediterranean near Sidon in Lebanon, a boat is built while neighbours drink coffee on the terrace.

46 (*above left*) Cotton is one of Syria's most important agricultural crops. Weighing a bale of cotton on a Syrian cotton plantation.

47 (*above right*) At the Syrian elections women have been given the vote.

48 (*below*) Many of the primitive ways of harvesting, such as those used by these reapers in northern Syria, have been replaced by modern methods.

49 Mechanical harvesters are now used in most places in Syria.

50 (*below left*) Modern industries such as glass manufacture thrive in Syria. This is a glass factory in Damascus.

51 (*below right*) An old Druze shaikh in Syria. The Druzes are a sect whose religious beliefs are secret and are only known to their elders, who pass through several stages of initiation.

52   Waterwheels have been used from time immemorial to raise water for irrigation from the River Al Asi, the classical Orontes, at Hama. They have now been replaced by mechanical pumps.

53   Oil is pumped to tankers through the pumping station. This one in the Syrian desert is on the Kirkuk-Mediterranean coast pipeline.

11 The cultivators

IT IS COMPARATIVELY EASY to write about the camel/breed/ing nomadic tribes for they constitute a single and definite type of culture from the Syrian desert southwards to central Arabia. To describe the way of life of farmers is more complicated, because it varies so greatly in different parts of the countries concerned. Firstly it is necessary to warn the reader that the term 'bedouin' is sometimes employed by city/dwellers as an expression of contempt for farmers and nomads alike – for anyone, that is to say, who does not today wear European clothes. In the present book, however, I have used bedouin only in the strict sense of camel/riding nomads.

When discussing the agricultural community, it is perhaps easiest to commence on the east, along the boundary of the desert and the town. In this area are situated a number of small tribes commonly classified as semi/nomadic, or perhaps as sheep/breeders, in contrast to the bedouin camel/breeders. Owners of large flocks of sheep suffer under some of the same disabilities as the bedouins. There is no room for them in the cultivated area in winter because all the land is under crops. In the desert, however, the rainfall is not uniform and thus, like the bedouins, they are obliged to seek out the areas where early autumn storms have enabled the grass to grow.

Whereas, however, camels can migrate for hundreds of miles and can go for several days without water, sheep can travel only short distances. Sheep/breeding tribes accordingly make use of donkeys as pack animals in place of camels. They migrate short distances into the desert, returning to the cultivated area in March for lack of water.

In many cases, these tribes own cultivation as well as sheep. Often in such semi/nomadic communities, the family will split up in winter, one brother taking the sheep out to the desert, while another remains on the farm or in the village. That this semi/nomadism is thousands of years old is illustrated by the story of Jacob and his sons. Jacob and his youngest son Joseph were living in Hebron, but the other sons had taken the family sheep to graze fifty miles away in Samaria.[13]

Until the 1920s, the great tribes of camel-breeding bedouins had from time immemorial dominated these areas on the verge of the desert and had often collected tribute from the semi-nomads. The latter, influenced by that human snobbery which causes the weak to imitate the strong, tended to look up to the bedouins and to imitate their manners and way of life. But since the aeroplane and the armoured car deprived the bedouin of his power, his social status has correspondingly declined.

As we move further westward and away from the desert, we find the cultivators living more and more in stone villages rather than in tents, although in certain areas such as the Jordan valley and the Kerak district, there are still static cultivators living in tents. The latter, in fact, possess certain advantages. In winter, for example, the tent can be moved to low ground sheltered from the wind, while in summer it can be pitched on a hill to catch cool breezes. Moreover, poor villages have few, if any, sanitary arrangements and in spring often suffer from fleas. A tent can be moved a few hundred yards to a clean site.

In these areas, the tribal structure of society still survives to a considerable extent. Tribes, like Trades Unions, are a form of association which men join to protect their interests. In theory each tribe is descended from one ancestor but, in fact, this is only true to a very limited extent. The villagers in Trans-Jordan and east Syria have been constantly recruited from nomadic tribes pushing in from the desert. When, however, a conquering tribe forced its way into an agricultural area, it was gradually absorbed by the original inhabitants, who were probably far more numerous than the conquerors. The name of the invading tribe was, however, retained for the resulting mixed population, only a small minority of which was really descended from the tribe in question.

The real and automatic solvent for tribal solidarity, however, is public security. As soon as law and order is thoroughly established, men leave the protection of their fellow-tribesmen and seek employment in cities or in other villages, where they possibly marry and lose their tribal affiliation. The cultivators are today in every degree of detribalization. It is so long since any kind of tribe existed in the Western Democracies that we are inclined to think of tribalism as an extremely primitive form of society. In fact, however, tribal organiza/ tion offers the tribesman considerable social benefits.

Within the tribe, no human being can die of hunger or exposure as was possible in the slums of great industrial cities in the West, at any rate until a few years ago. No child can be unwanted and have to be cared for in a state institution, as is still frequently the case in the Western Democracies. Tribal solidarity will support the widow, bring up the orphan, maintain the cripple or the invalid, all in the homely environment of their native village or camp. In tribal society, old people can never complain of loneliness.

We have already seen that the Ottoman system of government was to maintain large garrisons in the great cities, but to make little attempt to administer more remote tribal areas. As a result, the areas in the vicinity of cities were completely detribalized and the cultiva/ tors became individual farmers or just market gardeners, producing fruit and vegetables for the city.

West of the River Jordan, a few tribal names still survive but in general the unit is the village. The Lebanese coastal plain is in a similar state of development but in the mountains, less accessible to government authority, tribal and family ties are still strong. This is particularly the case among the Druzes, a minority community with a long history of struggle for survival.

Racially, as we have already seen, the cultivators are of very mixed origin. Apart, however, from such recent immigrants as the Cir/ cassians, it may be assumed that those east of Lebanon and of the River Jordan are predominantly of Semitic, that is to say of Arabian origin. West of the Jordan and in Lebanon, their origin is so mixed as now to be impossible to disentangle.

It has already been noted that, after the termination of the Crusades with the fall of Acre in 1291, European influence virtually disappeared for several centuries. During this period, the rural areas of Syro/Palestine became, superficially at least, almost entirely arabicized. One of the particularly Arab institutions in all villages was the guest house.

The Arab tradition of free and unquestioning hospitality for all comers, originally born in the desert, became transplanted to the villages of the cultivators. Any passer-by could sit down in the guest house and would find meals provided by day and bedding by night, and no questions asked. Sometimes the chief or headman of the village would keep open house, assisted behind the scenes by his relatives, at others the guest house would be a building held in common. At times, although the villagers dwelt in houses, the guest room would be a black tent.

If the visitor appeared to be a person of standing, carpets would be spread, on top of which mattresses, quilts and cushions would be laid out. The village elders would drop in to hear the news, discuss the state of the crops or other subjects of interest. The fire smoulder-ing on the hearth would be blown into flame and the coffee pots brought into action for a fresh brew. (Today, in the more 'civilized' villages in Palestine or Lebanon, the coffee may perhaps be made over a paraffin stove in the kitchen.)

Arab tradition lays down that a special animal has to be slaughtered for a distinguished guest. The custom is several thousands of years old as is attested by many references in the Bible.[14] In the desert and in the majority of Arab villages, the custom is still rigorously observed and a sheep or a lamb is killed for the visitor. Once again, however, more modern practices are gradually appear-ing in western districts.

Two obsessions of our civilization are time and money, both regarded in older traditions as of minor importance. The slaughter and cooking of a sheep occupies several hours and the resulting feast is out of all proportion to the possible appetite of the guests. In a few 'modern' villages, as a result, the visitor may be served with chicken, rissoles, kebabs and other small dishes. In Lebanon the meal may even be served on a table, the guests sitting on chairs.

To the old Arab idea of hospitality, anything less than the slaughter of a lamb or kid would show shameful parsimony. Not only must every guest be offered a banquet but the host must not eat with the visitor. On the contrary, the guests must eat alone, while the hosts remain standing ready to wait upon them.

172

In tribal society, the sheep slaughtered in his honour is served to the guest on a large dish or tray, on top of a mountain of rice, boiled wheat or bread soaked in gravy. The dish is deposited on the floor and the guests sit round it, eating with their hands. In the more sophisticated villages, spoons are sometimes provided.

To the American or European visitor, the sight of Arab tribes, men eating with their hands may seem disgusting and barbaric. In reality, these meals are controlled by a well-established code of manners. The guests are the first to eat. When they have finished, they are invited to wash their hands and sit down elsewhere for coffee. The host will then invite the more important men of the village or tribe to take the place of the guests at the dish.

At this stage, it is ill-mannered to show haste or eagerness. The polite will excuse themselves and suggest that others take their place before them. Among bedouins, who sit round in a circle and eat from the common dish, it is bad manners to stop eating before others have finished. Although he may himself have had enough, the tribesman will continue to pretend that he is still eating, taking very small mouthfuls, lest he embarrass those with larger appetites. Then, when all have had enough, the diners will rise together. Curiously enough, in villages a single man will sometimes rise and go off to wash his hands, leaving those still hungry to eat on.

The corollary of village hospitality was that no food shops existed in Arab villages nor could any food he bought for money. For the passer-by to buy food would have been an indelible disgrace on the village.

According to the most ancient tradition, land in Arab countries could not be privately owned. In the earliest ages, it was thought to belong to the local gods, subsequently to the one God. In Ottoman times, it was visualized as being the property of the government. The cultivators were originally the tenants of God and afterwards of the government.

In early times in the Arab countries, as in Europe, the land was farmed by the village as a community and every man was allotted his own strip to cultivate each season. After harvest, the land was re-divided before the next season. When agriculture became more advanced, this method ceased to be adequate. A man, for example, might want to plant fruit trees and, as a result, he wished to retain a plot of land as his own. Thus each villager became an independent farmer. The boundaries were known to the people of the village and, in the event of a dispute, the elders were called in to adjudicate.

During the latter half of the nineteenth century, the movement for modernization appeared in the Ottoman Empire. One facet of these reforms was to encourage private ownership of land, which would be registered in the government Lands Department, title deeds being given to the owner. In some areas, the cultivators were invited to register their lands but categorically refused. They regarded the government with intense suspicion and imagined that registration was a government trick to increase taxation or, even worse, to con-script their sons for the army.

Where the cultivators of large areas of farm land refused to register their holdings, corrupt Ottoman officials often sold title deeds to wealthy townsmen. A suitable sum of money, slipped into the palm of a Lands Department official, might purchase an estate of several thousand acres, already closely occupied and cultivated. To the purchaser, the deal was a gamble. If he could obtain soldiers to enforce his ownership, he compelled the cultivators in future to pay him a large share of the produce as 'rent'. If the government was unable to put him in possession, he kept the deed in his safe, hoping for better times.

The sale of agricultural land by the government preceded the execution of a cadastral survey on which the boundaries could be marked. It was not uncommon some years ago to find a perfectly legal Turkish title deed to a piece of land of which the boundaries were somewhat as follows: 'on the north the old mulberry tree, on the west the marsh, on the south Haj Muhammad's land and on the east the desert'. The whole story provided a sad example of the results which have often followed hasty and well-intentioned reforms imitated from Europe.

Another danger resulting from the attempt to regularize land ownership was the intervention of moneylenders. Farmers in every

174

country have good and bad years and periodically need credit to tide them over. Moneylenders for this purpose had existed in Syria for thousands of years. But as long as all the land belonged to God or the government, the moneylender could not deprive the farmer of his livelihood. In fact, in these simple times, a high standard of honesty was maintained between the parties. The merchant or moneylender advanced such sums as were necessary to enable the farmer to buy his seed or whatever else was needed and no documents were drawn up. At harvest time, the loan would be repaid either in cash or in wheat. The two parties to the transaction knew each other intimately and neither thought of appealing to the government, the police or the law-courts.

As soon, however, as the peasant received a title deed, the money-lenders obliged him to mortgage his land, demanded legal under-takings and sued him if he did not punctually repay his loan. When the moneylender foreclosed and obtained possession of the land, he normally did not evict the farmer but merely made him pay a large share of the produce to him as 'landlord', thereby further impoverish-ing the cultivators and enriching the city-dwellers. It was a surprising and distressing fact that the first result of the replacement of the ramshackle Ottoman administration by more legal and modern methods was to make the rich richer and the poor poorer.

Between the two world wars, the chaos which prevailed in the ownership of land under the Ottomans was largely cleared up by British and French experts. Detailed cadastral surveys were made, boundaries fixed, land registries were set up and title deeds issued. As a result, the situation in most respects became clear. This great and valuable administrative achievement did not, however, solve the problem of agricultural debt.

The theoretical ownership of the land by the government in Ottoman days should not be confused with modern theories of nationalization. The sole advantage of theoretical government ownership was that the law-courts were unable to order the sale of a farmer's land for debt. The Ottomans did not aspire to control agricultural operations, as modern communist governments have. Farmers are people of independent mind and normally work best if left to themselves. The Ottoman land law, however, did empower the government to take over cultivable land left persistently un-cultivated, a provision directed rather against the absentee landlord than the peasant farmer. The Ottoman authorities, however, rarely made use of these legal powers.

The problem of agricultural indebtedness is a common one all over the world. In India and in Egypt, to take two examples alone, British administrators in the past attempted to introduce legal measures to prevent farmers selling all their land. Surplus land could be disposed of, but when the farm had been reduced to the minimum size necessary to make it viable, the farmer was unable to dispose of the remainder. Such measures, however, were never entirely satis-factory.

The modern Western adviser will, of course, suggest an agricul-tural bank as the remedy, and these have indeed been opened by some Arab governments. In the present writer's experience, they did not operate with great success. Cultivators were often improvident and spent the money for other purposes, hoping not to have to pay it back. Consequently the bank demanded security before making a loan. The poor could not provide security with the result that the bank only lent to the rich.

Cooperative societies are not in general well suited to the intensely individualistic Arab temperament. Arabs, however, can be made to work together with enthusiasm, but to persuade them to do so is a social, even a spiritual task, rather than a financial one. Selfless and dedicated leaders, willing to live among them for purely altruistic reasons, could doubtless found and operate cooperative societies but such people are rare in any country.

It is true that, in recent years, 'socialist' parties in various Arab countries have attempted to break up large estates and to give the land to the cultivators themselves. Such measures, however, do not solve the problem of debt, for, as soon as the peasant obtains legal possession, he can mortgage the land to a moneylender.

Having been deeply interested in these problems for some thirty years, the writer is aware of their complexity. In Roman times, the imperial authorities gave the Greek cities of the Decapolis the power to rule the surrounding agricultural districts. There is little doubt that the city merchants exploited their subject peasantry as much as they could. Some people may shrug their shoulders and say that the peasants of these countries have always been serfs. To those unwilling to resign themselves to such a situation, the best hope may appear to be in the present rapid spread of education. To enable the villagers to defend themselves against exploitation may well be more bene-ficial than clumsy attempts at government intervention.

The present writer is obliged to admit to a bias in favour of the small, independent farmer rather than the big landlord. It must be admitted, however, that the advent of agricultural machinery has produced arguments in favour of the large landowner, the small farmer rarely being able to buy machinery. In many areas of Syria, Lebanon and Jordan, however, the land is so rocky and mountain-ous that only a very limited use can be made of machines.

In many areas where large landowners exist, share-cropping is still practised. Where the landlord provides the seed and the machinery or the animals, he will often divide the crop in half with the culti-vator or fellah. Where, however, the cultivator bears all the expenses, the landlord will probably receive only one quarter of the grain on the threshing floor.

Where the landlord takes part in the processes of agriculture, visits his land and provides machines or seed, his activities may be beneficial to all concerned. Nothing, however, can be said for the rich city-dweller who obtained title deeds through the favour or the corruption of the Ottoman officials, who was normally an absentee landlord and who sent an agent at harvest time to collect the 'rent'.

Most of the arable plains of Syria and Jordan lie east of the Lebanon mountains and of the River Jordan. The western face of the Lebanese mountains and of the hills of Samaria and Judaea are ideally suited to fruit growing. On the plains and in sheltered valleys, oranges and other citrus fruits will flourish and the Jordan valley produces bananas.

Higher up in the hills, vines, olives, figs, peaches, apricots and apples are extensively cultivated. Lebanon obtains a considerable revenue from the export of fruit. Jordan is less fortunate in that the state of Israel occupies the whole Mediterranean coast, preventing Jordan from exporting soft fruits to Europe. The establishment of a canning industry might enable Jordan to export her fruit more profitably, although she now sends both fruit and vegetables by air to the oil companies on the Persian Gulf.

While bedouins on the one hand and city-dwellers on the other often obtain most of the publicity, the cultivators constitute the large numerical majority of the people of Syria, Lebanon and Jordan. Their racial origin differs from the almost entirely Arab tribes on the fringes of the desert to the mixed populations of the Mediterranean coast and the occasional colonies of Circassians dotted about the Arab districts. Almost all, however, show the strong family feelings, the simple, country outlook and the ungrudging hospitality which renders them so attractive to those who know them.

12   The city-dwellers

SYRIA, LEBANON AND JORDAN include four of the world's
most remarkable cities, each characterized by peculiarities entirely
different from the other. These four cities are Beirut, the capital of
Lebanon, Damascus, the capital of Syria, Aleppo and Jerusalem.

Beirut is a city of the Mediterranean. The blue waters of the
Middle Sea lap its beaches, its harbour and its very houses, while the
Lebanese mountains, snow-capped in winter, stand at the end of
the streets like a theatrical backdrop. In few cities is it possible, as in
Beirut, to ski in the snows of Lebanon in the morning and to sun-
bathe on the Mediterranean beaches the same afternoon.

We are wrong, however, in thinking when we land in Beirut
that, being in Asia, we are now in the East. There is no hard and
fast line between East and West, and Beirut in many ways resembles
Greece and Italy more than it does Damascus – certainly more than
it does Baghdad. Its streets crowded with traffic, the prevalence of
European dress, the French shops, and the American accents, all
remind us that Lebanon from time immemorial has looked across
the sea. The international atmosphere, the blue sea and the lovely
mountains make Beirut one of the pleasantest towns in the world.

Damascus is different. Lying in a vast saucer of land, surrounded
on all sides by gardens which fade away into the blue distances of the
desert on the east, Damascus, seen from the hill of Salahiya, is as
beautiful as Beirut but in a very different way. One of the oldest
cities in the world, it has the distinction of being the only surviving
city mentioned in the Book of Genesis. Incidentally, of the small

towns still existing which are referred to in Genesis, Harran is in Syria and Hebron in Jordan.

In the modern district of Damascus, there are fine buildings and wide boulevards, but the Western visitor will probably find more interest in the covered bazaars or suqs, teeming with colourful throngs of townspeople, farmers and tribesmen. Here still survives the custom, observed also in mediaeval Europe, of grouping all the shops of one type together. The suq of the copper workers, the suq of the saddlers, the suq of the perfumers, each offer their various attractions.

Of the historical sites, the mosque of the Umayyads is impressive, in spite of the havoc wrought to the original building by Tamerlane. The Azem palace, now the Institute of Archaeology, enables the visitor to see how the great Damascus families used to live.

All through history, the people of Damascus have been famous for their turbulence, and they still maintain their reputation. Damascene politics are as bitter, emotional and violent as ever. The crowded coffee shops are the scene of many a vociferous argument and bitter denunciation of unpopular policies. All through the ages, moreover, the city has been famous for its xenophobia.

Aleppo, often in history a rival of Damascus, is more stolid and less mercurial, a city of merchants and of traders. For many cen-turies, the town was a centre for caravans carrying the rich commerce of Persia and the East to the markets of Syria and the ports of the Mediterranean. Sacked by Hulagu and subsequently by Tamerlane, it lost something of its splendour, but in the seventeenth century it was the most important centre in Syria for European businessmen. The Venetians, the French and the English Levant Company all operated in Aleppo, where the local merchants were more coopera-tive than those of xenophobic Damascus.

The commanding situation of the citadel of Aleppo is famous but the European visitor will probably be more interested in the bazaars or suqs, which here, unlike those of Damascus, still retain their old vaulting, dating back in part to the thirteenth century.

Jerusalem is once again a city of unique character, differing entirely from Beirut, Damascus or Aleppo. The old walled city, a

180

gem which has survived from the Middle Ages, looks over the hundred-yard-wide no man's land to the modern buildings and concrete flats of the new Israeli Jerusalem to the west. The interest of Jerusalem is, of course, religious. The old city is entirely surrounded by walls, approximately on the same alignment as in the time of Christ.

The temple area is now dominated by the beautiful building of the Dome of the Rock. Near by is the Church of the Holy Sepulchre, the Via Dolorosa and the Roman pavement believed to mark the place where Christ was tried before Pilate. Jerusalem, however, is so full of historical sites and associations that it cannot be described in this book.

The suqs of Jerusalem are in the crowded narrow streets of the old city, many of them going up and down steps, while the old houses on either side are joined by arches and buttresses overhead. The usual variegated crowds jostle through the narrow alleyways, though here they include tonsured monks, Roman Catholic, Orthodox, Coptic and Abyssinian priests and pious Muslim shaikhs telling their beads. Yet these very religious associations have made Jerusalem the scene of endless wars, massacres and fanaticisms. The barbed wire in the no man's land dividing the city today is in keeping with the whole history of Jerusalem.

'Thus fell and for ever the metropolis of the Jewish state', writes Millman,[15] describing the capture of Jerusalem by Titus. 'Other cities have risen on the ruins of Jerusalem and succeeded as it were to the inalienable inheritance of perpetual siege, oppression and ruin. Jerusalem might almost seem to be a place under a peculiar curse: it has probably witnessed a far greater portion of human misery than any other spot upon earth.'

The dwellers in the cities of Syria, Lebanon and Jordan may be arbitrarily divided for our purpose into two groups, the ruling, official and professional classes on the one hand, and the artisans, shopkeepers, taxi-drivers and craftsmen on the other. Such a division is obviously too rigid to be natural and the two groups melt into one another. Islam has never recognized castes or class distinctions and

181

all mix together with good humour in the streets and suqs. Nevertheless, their ways of thought are today often widely different.

The small shopkeepers and the poorer classes do not greatly differ
in their mental outlook from the inhabitants of the villages near the
city. In most cases sincere Muslims, their really basic loyalty is still
to their religion rather than to the nationalisms which have sprung
up in the last fifty years. The two loyalties, however, blend uncon-
sciously in their minds, for the enemies whom the politicians
denounce – the Western Powers, Russia or Israel – are none of them
Muslims.

These workers and shopkeepers are pleasant, simple folk,
hospitable and humorous. The majority also are extremely indus-
trious, and sit from sunrise to dark in their little shops for seven days
a week, closing only on Friday for a short time at midday to enable
them to join in the congregational Friday prayers. Their women,
with bourgeois respectability, play little part in public life but often
completely dominate the home.

Yet it is difficult to describe anything in the Arab world with
confidence, because conditions are changing so rapidly. What was
once called 'The Unchanging East' is now fast outstripping the
West in speed of change. The tremendous efforts expended on
education may transfer the sons of these good artisans and shopkeepers into the ranks of the intellectuals. Moreover, these city-
dwellers assiduously read the newspapers and but little else, and
listen to broadcasts. Urban populations are, at the same time, more
easily contacted by political propagandists than are villagers.

The second but more important group of city-dwellers are the
intellectuals, themselves now to some extent divided into age groups.
The years from the end of the First World War to 1945 or 1950 were
largely dominated by men brought up and educated under the
Ottoman régime. The Ottomans, as we have seen, maintained large
establishments in the big cities, where they achieved a reasonably
good understanding with the upper classes. The movement for Arab
independence, it will be remembered, was limited to a small number
of secret societies before the First World War.

After the departure of the Ottoman Turks, the upper-class Arab families were left in a commanding position. Many, as reasonable men, cooperated with the mandatory powers and attained responsible positions. Others went into opposition, though in Syria their action was political rather than military. Having been born under an empire which would brook no opposition, they may have considered that they were in no position openly to oppose a Great Power.

It will, moreover, be recollected that the self-appointed General Syrian Congress (in July 1919, before the allotment of the man-dates) had declared the need of the country for foreign advisers, though not for foreign domination.

The present writer worked for thirty years with and under Arab officials of this type and greatly enjoyed the association. Never once did he have a serious difference of opinion with his Arab colleagues or with the Cabinet ministers, who were his chiefs. Once they were convinced of the sincerity and devotion of a foreign official, they treated him with courtesy and cordiality. Personally I identified myself entirely with my Arab colleagues and often found them easier to deal with than British officials.

There were, however, two directions in which my viewpoint differed from theirs. Of these the first was their attitude to tribesmen and villagers. In this respect, though all now of course declared themselves to be Arabs, they seemed to have inherited much of the Ottoman attitude of hostility and contempt. To some extent, this attitude seemed to be a deliberate pose. On a number of occasions, I was requested by an Arab Cabinet Minister or senior official to interpret between them and some tribesman brought to their offices. 'I really cannot be expected to understand these primitive types,' the Minister would remark.

In one other direction, their views seemed to me erroneous and that was in their cynical misapprehension of the policies of Western nations. To some extent, such an attitude was comprehensible. Power politics, as practised by all nations, is often unscrupulous. Their estimate, however, while understandable, happened to be wrong and this was a handicap to success. Human motives and incentives are always immensely complicated and no policy, especially in modern Western states, is due to a single motive.

To adopt the view, therefore, that everything done by Western nations may be attributed to greed, treachery and a lust for power, is not a crime but a mistake. The United States and Britain, for example, while in some respects their policies can be attributed to selfishness, arrogance and economic incentives, are, in other directions, profoundly idealistic, sentimental and philanthropist.

The assumption that Western action was invariably dishonest and unscrupulous caused the Arabs to make many mistakes such as the refusal to give evidence before commissions genuinely appointed to ascertain the truth. The Arab boycott of debates on Palestine in the General Assembly of the United Nations was another case in point.

Since the Second World War, and particularly since 1950 and 1952, the situation has undergone a considerable change as the result of the supersession of the between-the-wars generation of politicians and officials. The older generation maintained control just long enough to see the complete evacuation of Syria, Lebanon and Jordan by foreign troops. Then, ironically enough, they were driven from power by younger men. Denounced as the 'stooges of imperialism', many were branded as traitors and a number were assassinated.

Human actions, as already remarked, are never due to one motive and are often so complicated as to be impossible to disentangle, even by the actors. To elucidate and classify the psychological phenomena which have torn Middle Eastern peoples since the Second World War is still an impossible task. The following comments can only be tentatively offered, at least to illustrate the complexities involved.

1 The men now in power, or struggling to achieve it, were born and brought up between the wars and reached adolescence just before or during the Palestine débâcle. They were thus deeply impressed with hatred of the West at their most impressionable age. Their predecessors, on the other hand, had been born and educated under the Ottomans.

There is, however, a twenty- or thirty-year interval, after any generation has acquired its prejudices at its impressionable age, before the same generation achieves power, by which time many of its acquired hatreds and devotions are already out of date. This would account for the fact that the generation which grew up in the 1940s are strongly anti-Western, although the Western Powers have now ceased to exercise any influence in their countries.

2 Between the wars, Russia enjoyed no prestige in Arab countries. This was only partly due to the presence of French and British forces. It also came from the openly anti-religious views disseminated by the communists and from their persecution of Muslims in their own territories. Now, however, Russia has become respectable and her views, her weapons and her propaganda are welcomed.

3 To many governments in various parts of the world and particularly to the somewhat autocratic régimes which have prevailed in Syria, a foreign enemy is a useful scapegoat. The habit of blaming everything on the 'imperialists' was easily acquired and even after all visible evidence of such persons has disappeared, still proves a useful asset.

4 Curiously enough, many of the symptoms shown by the younger generation in Syria today are simultaneously characteristic of the Western nations. Such phenomena are the revolt against parental, and indeed against all authority. Another symptom is the loss of pride in the past history of the nation. In Britain, many young people criticize or blame their forbears for having built up a worldwide empire. Arab friends have asked the present writer why he writes books about Arab history. 'What is the use of history?' they ask. 'If you want to help, why don't you write on the politics of today?'

Perhaps the desire to abolish titles, classes and privileges has also spread from Britain to the Arab countries and has influenced young Syrians in the denunciation of the alleged ineffectiveness, or corruption, of the previous generation of politicians, most of whom belonged to 'old' families.

5 Many thousands of students from Lebanon, Syria and Jordan go abroad to study every year. A proportion of these remain abroad, especially Christians. Students returning from Western universities differ considerably in their attitude, some remaining friendly to the country in which they studied, others resentful. The apparent sexual laxity in the West frequently gives rise to criticism, sometimes to contempt, but occasionally elicits approval.

Perhaps a guess may be hazarded that in general students returning from Western countries are:

(a) Passionately desirous to achieve in their own countries the high material standards of living which they have seen.

(b) Critical of what they believe to be the low spiritual level of Western nations and of their sexual laxity and lack of dignity.

(c) Unchanged in their views of the immorality of Western governments, perhaps because their fellow students in Western nations are themselves in semi-revolt against authority.

These speculations are little more than guesses regarding trends and should not be pressed too far.

Other trends developing, especially in Syria, where the Baath party now in power (1967) calls itself socialist, take the form of statements in favour of the abolition of poverty and want, and the right to every citizen to a living. Such objectives are almost verbatim repetitions of similar political slogans in the West.

The Syrians seem thus to be connected by a kind of love-hate relationship with the West. While denouncing France, Britain and the United States in the bitterest possible terms, they also adopt a great part of their own ideology from European socialist models.

But with this tendency towards socialism and nationalization, there is a growing disillusionment with Western democracy, once greatly admired in the Arab countries. The young intellectuals regard themselves as an *élite*, whose duty it is to lead the masses and direct them, if necessary by force, rather than to consult them.

Some of the younger intellectuals proclaim more drastic and revolutionary opinions. The whole social system they declare to be rotten. Everything must be swept away. An unfortunate aspect of revolutionaries in all countries is their concentration on the destruction of the existing institutions of which they disapprove, without a very clear idea of how they will be replaced. The result often is to impose on the nation a period of ten, fifteen or twenty years of intense hardship, before a new system can be substituted.

The alternative to complete revolution is the gradual introduction of reforms on the basis of existing forms, the valuable being retained and the unsuitable discarded. To some extent, Jordan represents the method of reform, Syria that of revolution, though both are aiming at the modernization of their countries.

The increasing power of intellectuals may be traced today in the Western nations as well as in Arab countries, and the two movements may well be connected. While Syrian intellectuals are extremely brilliant, they are inclined to indulge in theories rather than in facts. When they achieve political power, they are unable to carry through in practice the ideas which they had conceived in the realms of thought. Ideas seem to be to them more important than facts, or perhaps rather, they are so completely absorbed in ideas that they forget to consider facts. They are thus inclined to be carried away with the idea of the reconstruction of the mighty Arab Empire of a thousand years ago or with the vision of the Arabs triumphantly sweeping Israel into the sea, without pausing to consider whether they possess the means of executing the plans of which they dream.

In Syria, the failure of the intellectuals to control the situation when they achieve power opens the way for military rule. Western commentators, when offering their various opinions on Arab affairs, seldom make allowance for the difference between large and small nations. In such small countries as Syria, Lebanon and Jordan, everyone knows everyone else, prominent people are often related and local and family loyalties play an important part in public affairs.

The officers of the army in Syria come in general from the same small intelligentsia as the politicians. As a result of the great prestige attached among these people to academic achievement, a university degree is considered the best qualification for an army career. Even, however, where the army officers are largely recruited from intellectuals, a brief period of army service induces a certain practical form of mind. The failure of the pure intellectual at actual government thus often proves an irresistible temptation to the soldiers. A quick and usually bloodless *coup d'état* replaces the intellectuals by a military government.

We may, therefore, surmise that Syria is possibly tending towards a form of government with the following peculiarities:

(*a*) An equalitarian system, free from hereditary privileges, claiming to act for the good of the whole nation but not seeking the will
of the nation. A government claiming to be for the nation but not
by the nation.

(*b*) More often than not, the head of such a government will be a
soldier.

If this conjecture be true, the Syrians, bearing aloft the political
slogans of the West, will have unwittingly returned to the time-
honoured system of government of the Arabs – benevolent dictatorship with a military flavour. Ironically enough, Jordan, allegedly
the bitter ideological enemy of Syria, is practising the same system.

54 Cedar was an important commodity for the Phoenicians. The few remaining cedars of Lebanon, relics of an earlier age, are now a great tourist attraction.

55 The beautiful mountainous scenery of Lebanon is seen in this view of the Kadisha valley from the cedars.

56 The desert is parched and dry in summer but in spring the valleys are carpeted with grass and wild flowers.

57 The mountain ranges of Lebanon receive a good rain supply and even snow in the winter months.

58 Semi-nomadic tribes of cultivators, breeders and farmers live in
villages like this one in the Lebanese
mountains.

59 A corner of the battlements of
the crusader fortress of Crac des
Chevaliers, where once the Knights
Hospitallers paced on guard. Beyond
the castle walls, the hills are terraced
for vines.

60 (*left*) Byblos, the modern Jubail, was a thriving port two thousand years before Christ and exported cedar wood to Egypt. A Christian priest of the Orthodox Church walks through the silent streets of Byblos.

61 (*below left*) This is a courtyard in Aleppo, Syria, a city of merchants, traders and shopkeepers.

62 (*above right*) Scanty rainfall makes some degree of nomadism essential to Arab stock raisers. These people are semi-nomadic shepherds from the Judaean desert east of Bethlehem.

63 (*below right*) The black tent, associated with the Arab for thousands of years, is made of long woven strips of goathair stitched together and is supported on poles and held up by ropes. 'I am black but comely, O ye daughters of Jerusalem, as the tents of Kedar . . .' says the Song of Solomon.

64 The narrow vaulted streets of the old city of Jerusalem have changed little since the time of Christ.

65 An old shoemaker in one of the streets of Aleppo. In the sunny climate of Syria he can work out of doors for most of the year.

66 Local produce is still sold
from mobile stalls like this one
in Damascus.

67 In the modern quarters of
Damascus, the streets have an
up-to-date appearance.

68   A block of modern flats in Beirut, Lebanon.

69   The Syrian Protestant College of Beirut was founded by American missionaries in 1866. Now called The American University of Beirut, it is one of the most important centres for academic learning in the Middle East.

13   Historical experience and forms of government

FROM THE EARLIEST HISTORICAL TIMES down to our own, Syria and Jordan have always been autocratically ruled. It is a mistake to assume that autocracy is old-fashioned and that republicanism is modern. The Roman Republic endured for centuries before Christ and was followed by imperial autocracy. But in the later Middle Ages and the Renaissance many cities of Italy were again republics. The Greek cities were republics, followed by autocracy. In Europe the pendulum seems to swing back and forth between autocracy and democracy.

But in Syria, since the beginning of history, republicanism has never taken root. Moreover, this was not due to the backwardness of the country. As we have seen, for four thousand five hundred years out of five thousand, Syria has been more civilized than Western Europe. Twice Syria has been the capital of empires of world importance, the Seleucid and the Umayyad. Perhaps, therefore, we may suspect that there are factors other than sheer backwardness, which have caused the Syrians, for five thousand years, to reject republican and adhere to autocratic forms.

The principal reason would appear to lie in the quick intelligence and emotions of the people. The successful implementation of Western democracy requires a great measure of patience. If the opposing political party wins an election, we must watch it for five years ruin the country (in our opinion) before we can redress the balance. No Syrian would be so patient or so lethargic. As soon as he saw things going wrong (according to his views), he would join a conspiracy to overthrow the government by force. Edward Gibbon, with remarkable perspicacity seeing that he wrote in Lausanne, remarked that the Arab is *personally* free. He is not interested in majority rule. The majority may well be wrong but every Syrian is sure that *he* knows how things should be done.

In spite of all that the politicians tell us, nations do not choose their own governments, as a woman chooses a new dress in a shop. In course of time, unsuitable systems cause confusion and are dis-carded and only those systems which work are retained. When, therefore, a nation has for five thousand years made use of certain methods of government, there is a considerable probability that the system in question is suited to the character of the people.

The Muslim conquest in the seventh century added certain features to the local ideas of government. Let us for a moment consider what they were.

The caliph, the new ruler, was a member of the Prophet's family and thus enjoyed religious as well as political prestige. This factor strengthened his authority, though it was not strong enough to eliminate the usual Arab civil wars. His connection with the Prophet, moreover, made the public expect him to be pious and moral and thus did indeed result in an improvement in the standards of government.

The caliph maintained a civil government, with departments and civil servants much as we know them. But after the assassination of the Caliph Mutawakkil in 861, the Turkish mercenaries seized power, later to be followed by Saladin and his family, the Ayoubids, who were originally Kurdish mercenaries. The Ayoubids were succeeded by the Mamelukes, likewise a purely military system. The Ottomans, who followed the Mamelukes, were a military empire, even if local governors were not always soldiers. Thus Syria has been accustomed to military rule ever since 861, that is for over a thousand years.

In addition, there is a very fundamental reason why military rule is easily accepted in Muslim states. The Prophet, we have seen, declared that Muslims killed in war against non-Muslims received instant admission to Paradise. The result was that, throughout Muslim history, soldiers have been some of the most religious citizens. This is in complete contrast with Christian countries, where they have often been regarded as both brutal and impious.

This contrast still exists. In Christian countries, military intervention in internal disturbances is normally bitterly resented. In Muslim countries, the army is usually more popular than the politicians. Soldiers are visualized as pious, honest men. Military rule is expected to be more moral and less corrupt than civil. Western observers who lament the abandonment of 'representative government' in favour of military dictatorship are usually unaware of these special factors.

In the West, the past history of Europe, together with a certain amount of oversimplified propaganda, has resulted in the belief that there are two forms of government – autocratic oppression and democratic freedom. The Arab tradition cannot be classified in either of these categories.

The system of government employed by Muhammad's first successors or caliphs was a simple one. The caliphate was not hereditary, though it was recognized that the caliph must be a member of the Prophet's family. He was chosen as the most suitable man to rule. He enjoyed no pomp or ceremony or attributes of royalty. He was an ordinary citizen and was expected to walk about the town and talk to the citizens – yet he enjoyed absolute power.

When the caliphs moved to Damascus and became the rulers of a great empire, these simple customs were inevitably modified. The caliph had to have a bodyguard and could no longer meet and converse with all his people, but the principles have survived to this day.

The basis of traditional Arab rule is the accessibility of the man in authority. Originally the caliph was personally accessible to all his subjects. When the empire became too large, the local governor became a miniature caliph. For many hours every day, he sat in an open audience hall or in the public square of the city and everyone, down to the poorest and the most humble, was entitled to speak to

199

him, man to man. Moreover, the governor took immediate action. If the case required investigation, the appropriate official was sent off with the complainant to conduct the necessary inquiries and report back. If no investigation were needed, he gave his decision at once and it was immediately enforced. The tradition still survives, perhaps subconsciously, among Arab people. Between the two World Wars, British officers who served in Arab governments noted with surprise, perhaps with impatience, that not even the humblest Arab would be put off with an interview with a junior official. Every Arab believed himself entitled to see the top man, the king, the prime minister or the governor.

We see, therefore, that the theory of Arab rule differs from any pattern of government familiar to Europe. One-man rule, they have found, is more efficient than assemblies and committees, but the man who rules must give himself no airs, must be accessible to the meanest citizen and must be prepared to answer his questions.

In Europe, royal government is connected in our minds with a hierarchy of aristocrats, dukes, counts, earls and barons, each with hereditary rights. In Arab countries, no such organization has ever existed. There have never been titles or class distinctions.

The traditional form of government is, therefore, that of one man, chosen as the best candidate available, who has autocratic powers but should be accessible to all his subjects, among whom there should be no class distinctions.

This theory sounds plausible but the catch lies in the phrase, 'chosen as the best candidate available'. Among so emotional, so intelligent and so hasty a people, different groups were liable to support different candidates, and that probably by violent methods. It was under these circumstances that hereditary succession crept in.

As already suggested, nations do not choose their forms of government by a calm mental process, weighing the pros and cons of various systems. In practice, forms of government are hammered out through struggle, by assassination, civil war or riot. People who have seen their country thus ravaged are only too anxious to accept the son of the former ruler, crying, 'for Heaven's sake do not let us have any trouble.'

The Arabs had a modified form of heredity dating from before Islam. A leading family was accepted as paramount, but the best member of the family was chosen, not necessarily the eldest son – or even any of the sons – of the previous chief. This considerably modified form of heredity was adopted for the Arab caliphate.

At the end of the First World War, the Western Allies enjoyed immense prestige and their systems of government were admired and imitated. In Syria and Lebanon, the French introduced a republican system on the model of their own. In Trans-Jordan, the British organized a constitutional monarchy. These systems survived until the end of the Second World War owing to the continued presence of Western forces.

When the Allied armies withdrew in 1946, these institutions were for the first time put to the test. The result seems to emphasize once again a peculiarity already well known to persons interested in Arabs. A severely practical and individualistic people, they realize that the success of government depends on the men who rule, not on academic theories. This viewpoint has been largely lost in the West, where supreme importance is now attached to the theory of government and little thought is expended on finding good men to operate it.

The Arab attitude is the reverse. They are basically indifferent to vague conceptions such as socialism or democracy but they take an intense and passionate interest in the persons of their rulers. Jordan is still a constitutional monarchy and Syria a republic, but these outward forms are not of major importance. The stability of any Arab country depends on whether or not suitable personalities emerge as rulers.

The existence of a ruling family doubtless adds a measure of stability. But if the monarchy survives in Jordan, the fact will not be due to the royalist convictions of the people but to the personalities of the kings. Syrian stability will not depend on whether the country remains a republic but on whether a national leader can emerge who will be capable of ruling.

Lebanon as usual differs in this respect from the other countries. The mixed ethnic origin of the Lebanese and their association with the West from time immemorial seem to enable them to maintain a republican form of government. Such a system in other Arab countries rarely ensures stability unless, as in Egypt, it produces a personality who rules as an autocrat under a nominally republican constitution.

14   Manners and customs

THE MANNERS AND WAY OF LIFE of the people of Syria, Lebanon and Jordan vary from the completely Westernized to the traditional Arab, unchanged for many thousands of years. The most Westernized city in any of the three countries is Beirut, where modern hotels, cabarets, night clubs and bathing beaches are to be found in abundance. Many of the leading inhabitants live under completely Westernized conditions, some with a French and others with an American flavour. The more flashy and meretricious features of Beirut are intended to cater for tourists, both from the West, and from Egypt, Iraq, Saudi Arabia and other Arab countries.

In other cities of the three countries, the official and professional classes and the rich merchants live under semi-European conditions. For example, their houses are furnished with tables and chairs, beds, dressing-tables and cupboards. In Muslim houses, the front door usually leads to the reception room, which is commonly used by men. A separate door from the entrance hall or beyond the reception room, leads to the domestic apartments, kitchen, perhaps dining-room and bedrooms. Arabs are extremely hospitable and often keep open house for men in their reception room. Arab lady visitors, however, are shown directly into the domestic apartments and do not enter the men's guest room.

European or American women, if they arrive with their male relatives, will sit down at first in the men's room. After a short time, the Western ladies can then ask the host if they may visit his family. He will probably retire for a few minutes to warn the ladies, after which the visitors will be shown into the domestic apartments. Arab men do not assist their wives in cooking, washing-up or other domestic duties. Any attempt to do so would probably meet with vigorous opposition on the part of the women.

Among poorer people with very small houses, the complete segregation of the sexes is impossible for lack of space, and the two- or three-roomed house and possibly a court-yard also, will normally be occupied by children and domestic utensils, with several women hurrying to and fro. Male visitors who knock on the door should wait. If only female voices reply and the visitor does not know Arabic, he will be well-advised to go away and try again later when the men are at home. For male visitors to enter a house occupied only by women would be highly objectionable.

If the husband be at home, the male visitors should still wait out-side the door, as time should be allowed for the women to collect the children and retire to one room, while the men receive the visitors in another room. Should the male callers accidentally see a woman hurrying across the court-yard or in a room with an open door, they should hastily look the other way. It is considered extremely offensive for men to stare at or to try and catch a glimpse of the women.

Such are the traditions of Arab life. On the other hand, among the Westernized and official classes, women now sometimes accompany their husbands to dinners and cocktails. When in doubt, however, it is best to assume that women will not join the party, leaving the initiative to the family. Christian Arab women may be slightly more ready to appear than are Muslim women, but even with Christians, unless completely Westernized, women will normally remain some-what in the background.

Among Muslims, it is not considered polite for strange visitors to inquire after the female members of the family. If the visitors are already friends, inquiries may possibly be permitted. The correct formula is then to ask after 'the family', not 'your wife'. Women should never be referred to by their first names, unless they are relatives or servants. On the other hand, small children often come in to greet the visitors and should be welcomed and spoken to kindly, for Arabs are extremely fond of children.

In villages or in the tents of nomads, there will sometimes be no furniture. The guest room or tent will be spread with coloured rugs or carpets, with mattresses, quilts and cushions laid round the walls for people to sit on. The centre of the room will be empty, the guests sitting all round with their back to the walls. When food is served, it is brought either in one large dish or in a number of plates, and is placed on the ground in the centre of the room.

The guests are then invited to sit round and eat. Normally the guests eat alone but they may invite their host to join them. Some refuse, considering it the duty of the host to wait upon the guests. Before and after food, a jug and basin are brought round for the guests to wash their hands. When eating without spoons or forks, only the right hand should be used.

Western visitors often find extreme difficulty in sitting on the ground. It is not good manners to extend the legs, to stick them out into the centre of the room or tent or to show the soles of the feet. The best way normally to sit on the floor is tailor-wise, cross-legged. However, the visitor need not be unduly alarmed. Most villagers and even bedouins are now accustomed to Western visitors. Incidentally, it is impossible for ladies in short skirts to sit gracefully on the ground. If an occasion of this kind is likely to arise, it is advisable to wear trousers or perhaps to have a long overcoat.

Muslims are not permitted to drink intoxicants though many Westernized Arabs do so. On the whole it is best not to suggest drink until the host does so. In tribes and villages, alcohol may give serious offence and should not be produced.

All Arabs, of whatever rank, are extremely polite. Precedence is considered by them to be of importance. Even among Westernized Arabs, there is a tendency to arrange all the chairs round the walls in a reception room, instead of scattered around facing different ways, as in Western countries.

This formal arrangement normally includes one or two seats, usually in the middle of one side or one end, which are the most important. It is usually obvious, when entering a room, which are the most important seats. If the room be empty, the visitors will be shown to the 'best' seats and the members of the family will arrange themselves on either side. If important persons subsequently come in, the visitors may go through the motions of vacating the best seats and going down lower.

In the same manner, when entering a room in which a number of the seats are already occupied, it is polite for the visitor to try and sit on a seat at the bottom end of the room. The host will then urge him to take a better seat. The procedure is perfectly described in Luke xiv. 7–11.

When entering through a door, care should be taken to hang back and invite one's companion to pass in first. He will probably refuse but the necessary courtesies will thereby have been satisfied. In the same way, if coffee or cigarettes be passed round, it is polite to invite one's neighbour to help himself first. As in Europe, the right-hand seat is the more honourable. When travelling by car, one's companion should be invited to sit on the right. Similarly, when walking down the street, the other person should walk on the right. When seated in a room, it is polite to stand up when other persons enter. If the new visitors appear to be greeted as important people, it may be polite to offer one's seat and attempt to move down lower.

Titles vary greatly in different communities. Among officials and important townspeople, such titles as 'Your Excellency' and 'Your Honour' are freely used in Arabic. When speaking English, it is well to note what titles are being used by others present. In any case, important officials such as Cabinet Ministers, Provincial Governors or Ambassadors should be addressed as Your Excellency. In tribes and villages, on the other hand, no titles are used and an equalitarian atmosphere usually prevails.

Dignity is a natural quality to Arabs. It is bad manners to shout, to laugh loudly or to play the fool in public. They will not lean back and laugh with their mouths wide open, as do Western peoples. All Arabs are particular about dress. Officials will normally wear a suit, collar and tie. Shorts, as often worn by Westerners, are considered undignified for men as well as for women. Full-length trousers should normally be worn.

All Semitic peoples are extremely unwilling to expose their bodies.

Men will often be unwilling to undress even before men. Scanty clothing for women is regarded as lacking in modesty as well as in dignity. The respect felt by Arabs for even the greatest nations is often greatly reduced by the lack of dignity of their citizens, both in the direction of noisiness, boisterous conduct and undignified attire.

In spite of the admiration they feel for courtesy and dignity, Arabs are normally extremely equalitarian. All classes of society are willing to join in conversation at any time and are usually pleasant and welcoming.

Shopkeepers are usually prepared to bargain and it is not essential, especially in gift shops, to pay the price first asked. It is not, however, necessary to shout or gesticulate. To say, 'I cannot afford so much', and then move quietly on, will probably result in a lower bid.

Some historic mosques are open to non-Muslim visitors, others are not. Careful inquiries should be made before attempting to enter, which should normally be done only with a Muslim attendant or guide. Arabs remove their shoes when entering a place of worship and Europeans should do the same. In some places, however, slippers are provided which can be worn over the shoes.

Most Western visitors are extremely ignorant of the Muslim religion and even regard it as some dark heathen superstition. Islam is, in reality, founded on Judaism and Christianity and has sometimes been called merely a Christian heresy. The Prophet Muhammad called Jesus Christ 'The Spirit of God', and acknowledged the Virgin Birth. Hostility between Islam and Christianity throughout the centuries was largely political, the result of the early Arab conquests of Syria, Palestine, Africa and Spain and, later, of the Crusades. In matters of religion, Arabs have always been extremely tolerant and have never persecuted either Jews or Christians.

Muslims are divided into two groups, Sunnis and Shiites. The original cause of the split was the rivalry between the different branches of the Prophet's family. Those who supported the Ummayads and the Abbasids were Sunnis, while those who favoured Ali and his descendants were called Shiites. The two branches, however, with the passing of the centuries, have now also become divided on certain points of dogma and ritual.

The great majority of the Muslims in Syria are Sunnis. There are Shiites in southern Lebanon called Mutawalis. Near Selemiya, east of Homs, is a community of Ismailis, who are followers of the Agha Khan. Southeast of Latiqiya, another heretic Muslim sect is the Nusairis. Reference has already been made to the Druzes.

Muslims are supposed to pray five times a day, before sunrise, at noon, in the afternoon, at sunset and at night. These statutory prayers are intended for praise and adoration, not for addressing personal requests to God. A different Arabic word is used for supplications.

The Muslim year differs by ten days from the calendar year and thus the Muslim months do not always come at the same season. In the month of Ramadhan, Muslims are forbidden to eat, drink, smoke or indulge in similar pleasures from first dawn to sunset. When Ramadhan comes in mid-summer, this imposes a heavy strain, especially on persons obliged to do physical labour in the sun. The Lesser Feast comes at the end of Ramadhan. The Greater Feast, which falls on the 10th of the month of Dhu al Hijja, is the day of pilgrimage outside Mecca.

Both feast days provide the occasion of public holidays, swings and roundabouts are set up in the streets, children appear dressed in bright new clothes and friends call upon one another to exchange greetings.

Christians are divided into various sects and churches in the same way as Muslims. Over the whole area, the majority of Christians belong to the old Eastern or Orthodox Church. In Lebanon, the greater part of the Christians are Maronites, a seventh-century heresy from the Orthodox Church. In 1736, however, the Maronites accepted the supremacy of the Pope, though remaining a separate community. American, Anglican and German missions have, in the last hundred years, founded small congregations of Protestant churches at various places.

Arabs in general are pleasant, well-mannered and cheerful. They are extremely hospitable, make warm-hearted and devoted friends and are normally remarkably tolerant. They have never used persecution or torture against minorities, as was once done so commonly in the West. They are, however, easily excitable and are inclined to be jealous of one another. They tend to visualize government as the rule of one man and they are not greatly moved by such vague conceptions as socialism or communism.

Under a strong leader, the Arabs have repeatedly played an important role in history but, in the absence of a capable ruler, they tend to be politically unstable. The people of Damascus are particularly known for political volatility.

Western visitors should always behave with politeness and observe the conventions in their dress and behaviour. It is essential to avoid both condescension and forced or undignified familiarity. It is undesirable to seek to gain favour by speaking with contempt or with criticism of other Western and Christian nations, a course which does not impress the Arabs. Avoid politics at all costs, do not tell people patronizingly that they should adopt Western democracy – be pleasant, cheerful and polite, as dealing with equals. Western tourists who complain of receiving rudeness have often themselves been guilty of it. A smile is often the best passport.

PUBLISHER'S NOTE

This book was completed before the outbreak of hostilities in June 1967. Sir John's views on these recent events and the general situation in the Middle East are set out in a pamphlet 'The Middle East Crisis'.

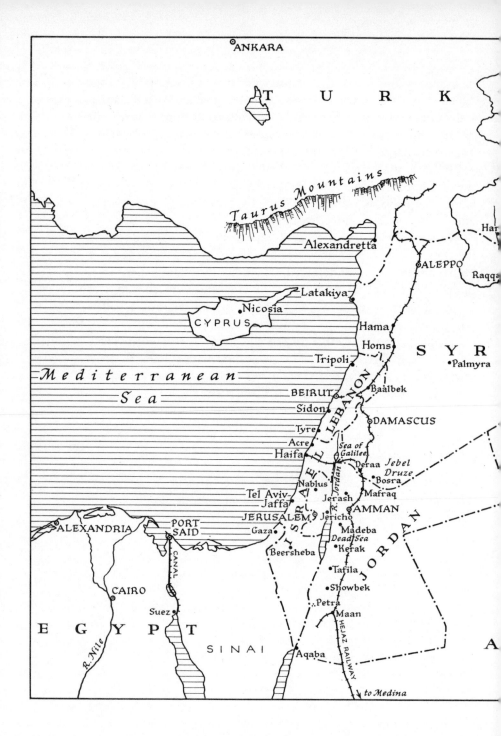

Y

L.Van

Diyarbekr

Nisibin

Mosul

Euphrates

R. Tigris

Habbaniya

Ramadi

BAGHDAD
Ctesiphon

Kerbela

I R A

Hilla

Diwaniya

Q

Kut

L.Urmia

•Hamadan

I R A N
(P E R S I A)

Caspian
Sea

Amara

Abadan

BASRA

U D I

B I A

Kuwait

| 0 | 50 | 100 | 150 | 200 | 250 Miles |
| 0 | 100 | 200 | 300 Km. |

VII   *Syria Lebanon Jordan today*

Notes on the text

1 GEOGRAPHY, CLIMATE AND EARLY INHABITANTS

1 See for example Genesis xxiii and xxvi.

3 FROM AUGUSTUS TO MUHAMMAD

2 The title of a colony in Roman times bestowed an honourable status and all the inhabitants became Roman citizens.

3 *See* Hitti, P.K., *History of Syria including Lebanon and Palestine*, London, 1951, p. 322.

5 THE CRUSADES

4 By a previous marriage, Fulk had been the father of Geoffrey Plantagenet, whose son was Henry II, King of England. Hence the royal families of Jerusalem and England became cousins.

7 SYRIA UNDER THE OTTOMAN EMPIRE

5 For this chapter see map VII, pages 210–11.

6 In Ottoman imperial days, senior officials, provincial governors, or commanders of divisions in the army, were given the rank of pasha, approximately corresponding to knighthood in Britain.

7 The Sublime Porte (or the Exalted Gate) was a title used for the Ottoman government.

8 Pronounced Hameed.

8 SYRIA BETWEEN THE WARS

9 Pronounced Shareef.

10 Sharif Husain of Mecca had meanwhile assumed the title of king.

9 UNITY OR DIVERSITY

11 Kerr, M., *The Arab Cold War*, London, 1960.

10 THE BEDOUINS

12 A wadi is a water course in the desert, normally dry, but which fills with water after rain.

11 THE CULTIVATORS

13 Genesis xxxvii. 12–14.

14 For example Genesis viii. 1–8.

12 THE CITY-DWELLERS

15 Millman, H.H., *History of the Jews*, ii, London, 1909.

Select Bibliography

NOTE I have limited this list to works in English, with one or two in French. Innumerable books have been published in the last fifteen years on the rapidly changing political situation in the Middle East. I have omitted these and confined myself to works of general, historical or cultural interest.

Abdullah, *Memoirs of King Abdullah of Jordan*, London, 1950.
Bell, G., *Amurath to Amurath*, London, 1911; *The Desert and the Sown*, London, 1907.
Belloc, H., *The Crusade*, London, 1937
Blunt, Lady Anne, *The Bedouin tribes of the Euphrates*, London, 1879; *A Pilgrimage to Nejd*, London, 1881
Buckley, C., *Five Ventures*, London, 1954
Bullard, R., *The Middle East. A political and economic survey*, London, 1950
Burton, Sir Richard, *A pilgrimage to Mecca and Medina*, London, 1913
Chair, S. de, *The Golden Carpet*, London, 1944
Creswell, K. A. C., *Early Muslim Architecture*, Oxford, 1932
Dearden, A., *Jordan*, London, 1958
Doughty, C. M., *Travels in Arabia Deserta*, London, 1921
Fedden, R., *Crusader Castles*, London, 1950; *Syria and Lebanon*, London 1965
Glubb, J. B., *The Story of the Arab Legion*, London, 1948; *The Great Arab Conquests*, London, 1963, New York, 1963; *The Empire of the Arabs*, London, 1963, New York, 1965; *The Course of Empire*, London, 1965, New York, 1966; *The Lost Centuries*, London, 1967
Grant, C. P., *The Syrian Desert*, London, 1937
Grousset, R., *Histoire des Croisades*
Haslip, J., *Lady Hester Stanhope*, London, 1934

Hitti, P.K., *History of the Arabs*, London, 1937; *History of Syria including Lebanon and Palestine*, London, 1951

Hourani, A.H., *Syria and Lebanon*, Oxford, 1946

Jarvis, C.S., *Arab Command*, London, 1942

Kirk, G.E., *A Short History of the Middle East*, London, 1948

Lammens, H., *La Syrie*, Beirut, 1921

Lane-Poole, S., *Saladin and the Fall of the Kingdom of Jerusalem*, London, 1898

Longrigs, S.H., *Syria and Lebanon under French Mandate*, Oxford, 1958

Middle East Survey 1965–1966 (for statistics), London (Europa Publications)

Muir, Sir William, *Annals of the Early Caliphate*, London, 1883; *The Mameluke or Slave Dynasty of Egypt*, London, 1896

Musil, A., *In the Arabian Desert*, London, 1931

Nicholson, R.A., *A Literary History of the Arabs*, London, 1914

Runciman, S., *A History of the Crusades*, Cambridge, 1951–5.

Appendix I: Statistics

THE HASHEMITE KINGDOM OF JORDAN

POLITICAL CONSTITUTION
Legislative power is vested in the King and the National Assembly, which consists of two houses, the Senate and the House of Representatives.

The House of Representatives is elected by secret ballot in a general election once every four years. The King has the power to dissolve the house before its term has ended.

The members of the Senate are appointed by the King, who also appoints the Prime Minister. Cabinet Ministers need not be members of either house but are entitled to speak in either.

AREA	96,000 square kilometres.
POPULATION	1,850,000, of whom 500,000 are classified as Palestine refugees.
AGRICULTURE	There are no large landowners in Jordan and most cultivators are small peasant farmers. Only twenty-two agricultural holdings exceed 2000 acres.
CROPS	West of the Jordan, land is limited and consists largely of terraced mountain slopes. Crops are wheat, barley, vegetables and fruit trees.
	East of the Jordan the land is more open but the rainfall is precarious. The principal crop is wheat, with barley in second place.
	Olive oil and fresh vegetables are exported.
FINANCE	Jordan is not financially self-supporting but hopes to be so by 1970. Until the abrogation of the Anglo-Jordan Treaty

216

in 1957, Britain made up the annual deficit in the budget. The Jordan budget for 1965–6 provided for an expenditure of 58·5 million Jordan dinars. (The dinar equals £1 sterling, $2·8.) Of this total, JD 22·7 million were allocated to development projects.

Revenue included JD 11·4 million from the United States and JD 1·4 million from Britain.

MINERALS   There are few minerals in Jordan.

In 1964, 842,000 tons of phosphates were produced.

It is hoped by 1969 to complete a project for the production of potash from the Dead Sea.

EDUCATION   Striking progress has been achieved in education.

In 1955, 226,030 students were studying in 1075 schools. In 1965, 386,071 students were studying in 1895 schools. More than 15,000 Jordanian students are studying in foreign universities.

The University of Jordan, founded in 1962, has 1138 students.

TOURISM   Jordan possesses unrivalled attractions for tourists in its religious and archaeological sites, its climate and scenery. In 1961, slightly over 150,000 tourists visited the country. In 1965, the number had increased to 500,000.

INDUSTRY   Industry in Jordan is very limited. Cement, phosphates, soap, tobacco and cigarettes are the chief items. There is an oil refinery in operation. Aqaba is Jordan's only seaport.

REPUBLIC OF LEBANON

POLITICAL CONSTITUTION

Legislative power is vested in one house, the Chamber of Deputies, which consists of ninety-nine members. They are elected by secret ballot on a religious, not a territorial basis. The allotment of seats to religions is as follows:

Maronite Christians	30
Sunni Muslims	20
Shiite Muslims	19
Greek Orthodox Christians	11
Greek Catholic Christians	6

Druzes	6
Armenian Orthodox	4
Armenian Catholics	1
Protestant	1
Others	1
	—
	99
	—

This provision in the constitution emphasizes how the Lebanese mountains have all through history provided a refuge for religious sects.

Executive power is vested in the President of the Republic, who is elected for a term of six years. He chooses his own ministers, who are not necessarily members of the Chamber of Deputies. The President himself can initiate laws.

AREA
: 10,400 square kilometres.

POPULATION
: 1,800,000 (1962).

AGRICULTURE
: Fruit is by far the most important agricultural product and represents one-fifth of Lebanon's foreign currency receipts from exports. Wheat is the principal grain crop. Agriculture employs slightly less than half the population.

FINANCE
: Visible imports to Lebanon greatly exceed exports. In 1964, exports totalled 209 million Lebanese liras (8·6 Lebanese liras equal £1 and $2·8), whereas imports were LL 1,328 million or more than six times the imports. The balance of trade is partly compensated by remittances from Lebanese residents abroad, by profits from the transit trade through the port of Beirut to Syria, Jordan and Iraq and from the profits arising from the fact that Beirut is the financial and commercial centre of the Middle East. Growing xenophobia in Egypt has resulted in the transfer of many foreign firms from Cairo to Beirut, where there are now (1967) more than eighty banks. In 1966, the estimated budget expenditure was LL 639·9 million (£74 million). Much capital development has been made possible by foreign aid.

INDUSTRY
: There are few manufactures in Lebanon. Vegetable oils, textiles, soft drinks and cement are exported. Several oil pipe-lines from Iraq and Saudi Arabia terminate in Lebanon and there are two oil refineries and four sugar plants.

218

| TOURISM | Tourism is important in the Lebanese economy. There are seventy large modern hotels in Beirut alone, some two hundred smaller ones and hundreds of hotels and pensions in tourist resorts in the mountains.
In 1965, Lebanon earned some LL 300 million from tourism, and was visited by some 700,000 tourists. |
| EDUCATION | The standard of education is higher in Lebanon than in any other Arabic-speaking country of the Middle East. In 1963-4, 145,491 pupils were studying in 1200 state schools and perhaps an equal number in private schools. There are three universities in Beirut. |

SYRIAN ARAB REPUBLIC

POLITICAL CONSTITUTION

The political instability of Syria has resulted in frequent changes of the constitution. Syria is described as a sovereign democratic popular socialist republic. The details of the constitution are still open to change and modification.

AREA	185,180 square kilometres.
POPULATION	5,399,000 (1964).
AGRICULTURE	Wheat is by far the most important crop, occupying half the total area under cultivation, the remainder being employed for barley, cotton, fruit and vegetables.
INDUSTRY	The principal industrial products are woollen fabrics and silk and cotton textiles. Raw cotton and cotton yarn are exported. Cement is manufactured and beer, wines and spirits.
FINANCE	Twelve Syrian liras are equal to £1; 4·3 Syrian liras are equal to $1.
In 1965, the Ordinary Budget was balanced at £S 710 million. Approximately half the expenditure was on National Security. In addition a five-year development plan (1965-70) will cost £S 2,780 million. Thirty-seven per cent of this amount will be spent on irrigation and agriculture, 25 per cent on industry, mines and petroleum, 23 per cent on transport and communications and 15 per cent on housing and public services.

Syria is on better terms with communist countries than are Lebanon or Jordan, and she has received loans for development purposes from Poland and East Germany. Sixty-four per cent of her cotton exports went to China, Rumania, Yugoslavia and other communist countries. In the period from 1961 to 1965, Syrian exports continued to rise and her imports to fall. Syria's political instability should not be allowed to conceal the fact that the country is progressing financially and commercially.

MINERALS Drilling for oil is in progress in northeast Syria, where oil reserves are believed to be considerable.

EDUCATION In 1963, there were in Syria 3887 primary schools, at which 578,692 pupils were studying.

Secondary schools were said to be 583 in number, with 116,619 pupils. There were two universities, with a total of 21,000 students.

TOURISM Tourism is not a major industry in Syria, as it is in Lebanon and Jordan.

Appendix II

A brief list of the principal places of historical or archaeological interest

JORDAN

Jerusalem   The old city of Jerusalem is entirely in Jordan.
The Church of the Holy Sepulchre.
The Temple Area, including
>The Dome of the Rock
>The Aqsa Mosque
>The Wailing Wall.

The Damascus Gate.
The Garden of Gethsemane.
The Mount of Olives.
Streets and bazaars in the Walled City.
Gordon's Calvary.
Jerusalem Museum.

Bethlehem   The Church of the Nativity.
The Tomb of Rachel.

Jericho   The mound of ancient Jericho.
The Dead Sea.
The Place of Baptism in the Jordan.

Amman   The present capital of Jordan, the Rabboth Ammon of the Old Testament. (The Philadelphia of the Greek period.)
Roman Theatre.
Citadel.

Jerash	An exceptionally well-preserved and excavated Graeco-Roman city, once one of the cities of the Decapolis.
Madeba	A small Christian town thirty-five miles south of Amman. Byzantine mosaic on the floor of the church.
Petra	The ruins of Petra, once the capital of the Nabataean kingdom, are unique. Situated in a cleft of the mountains, its most striking feature is the immense classical façades cut into the face of the cliffs.

LEBANON

Beirut	The capital of Lebanon. The population of the city is half a million, about one quarter of that of the whole country. Beirut is a modern tourist centre, with luxury hotels, night clubs and other holiday amenities. Its situation is delightful. It is also an active business city. Many Western firms, formerly centred in Cairo, have moved to Beirut. Beirut Museum deserves a visit.
Byblos	The modern Jubail, is only some fourteen miles north of Beirut and possesses many monuments from the earliest times. The historic inscriptions on the Dog River can be seen on the way.
The Cedars	are situated some seventy-five miles north of Beirut and can be visited in a day by road through Byblos and Tripoli. The drive is lovely, first along the Mediterranean coast and then through the mountains.
Beit al Din	is thirty miles from Beirut in the mountains. It is the former palace of the great Bashir al-Shihabi, Prince of Lebanon. The drive through the mountains is beautiful.
Tyre and Sidon	are names famous in the Bible and throughout history. There is little to be seen in these little towns but the drive is delightful.

SYRIA

Damascus   is one of the most ancient, historical and exciting cities in the world.
The Great Mosque of the Umayyads is splendid. Once a pagan temple, then a Christian cathedral, now a mosque, remains of all its past ages are visible.
The Azem Palace, now the Institute of Archaeology.
The Tekkiya.
The Museum.
The Bazaars, or suqs, should be visited.

Aleppo   is somewhat remote for tourists. Both the citadel and the roofed bazaars, or suqs, are impressive and well worth seeing.

Baalbek   lies in the Baqa valley between the Lebanon and anti-Lebanon ranges, and may be visited from Beirut or Damascus. The existing ruins, extensive and extremely impressive, are Roman. Baalbek was called Hierapolis by the Greeks and Romans and was a Roman colony. If possible, Baalbek should be visited in spring.

Crac des Chevaliers (Husn al akrad)   is a perfect Crusader castle, well restored during the time of the French mandate. Originally the property of Raymond, Count of Tripoli, it passed to the Hospitallers (the Knights of St John of Jerusalem) in 1142. There are many Crusader castles in Syria, but Crac des Chevaliers is the greatest and is also in better repair than any other.

Palmyra   is about 160 miles from Damascus by car. The ruins are extensive and a whole day can be well spent there.

Syria, Lebanon and Jordan are covered with historical monuments, dating from the Stone Age and the Bronze Age to modern times. These can be found in the guide books. Only a few of the most famous have here been mentioned.

Acknowledgments

Alinari, 7; M. Andrain, 12, 17; Artaud, 20; Berlin State Museum, 9; Black Star, 60; C. Bowers, 59; by courtesy of the Trustees of the British Museum, 3, 4; Camera Press Ltd., 19, 34, 35, 37, 38, 43, 47, 64, 67, 68, 69 (P.S. Dorrell, 21; Patellani, 26); J.A. Cash, 25, 40, 41, 42, 56, 58, 61, 65; by courtesy of Le Conseil National du Tourisme au Liban, 58; A. Duncan, 14, 22, 62, 63; by courtesy of the Embassy of the Hashemite Kingdom of Jordan, 32; from J.B. Glubb, *A Soldier with the Arabs*, London, 1963, by courtesy of the publishers: Hodder and Stoughton Ltd., 33; Imperial War Museum, 28, 29, 30, 31; The Mansell Collection, 27; by courtesy of the Trustees, The National Gallery, London, 6; Oriental Institute, University of Chicago, 5; P. Popper, 16, 39, 49, 50; M. Stafford, 8, 10, 11, 44, 45, 55, 56.

Who's Who

ABDULLA, HM King (Jordan; 1880–1951). Second son of Sharif (later King) Husain of the Hejaz. Amir of Trans-Jordan, 1921–46. King 1946–51. Assassinated in Jerusalem, on 20 July 1951. Founder of the state of Jordan.

AFLAQ, Michel (Syria; b. 1910). Damascus Christian. Educated Paris, Sorbonne. Taught history in colleges. Founded Baath Socialist Party with Akram Haurani and Salah Bitar.

ARSLAN, Shakib (Lebanon; 1869–1946). Member of aristocratic Druze family of Lebanon. Poet, author, politician. Member of Ottoman Parliament 1913–18. Exiled by French and lived in Switzerland. Editor of *La Nation Arabe* published in Geneva. Influenced nationalist sentiment in North Africa.

ATASI, Hashim (Syria; 1869–1960). Sunni Muslim from Homs. Educated in Istanbul and an official under Ottoman government. Nationalist leader during French Mandate. President of Republic 1936–39 under French. President 1950–51 and 1954–55.

ATRASH, Sultan (Syria; dates unknown). Member of leading family of Druzes in Jebel Druze. Leader of Druze rebellion against French in 1925.

AUDA abu Taya (Jordan; *c.* 1850–1925). A shaikh of the Huwaitat tribe. Famous as a fighter, he played an important part in the Arab revolt against the Ottoman government in the First World War in connection with Amir Feisal and T. E. Lawrence.

BITAR, Salah (Syria; b. 1912). Sunni Muslim of Damascus. Educated in Paris, then employed as a school teacher. Minister of Foreign Affairs 1956–58. Played a leading part in forming the United Arab Republic in 1959. Prime Minister on several occasions 1963–66.

HAFIDH, Amin (Syria; b. 1920). Sunni Muslim of Aleppo. NCO French forces in Syria. Commissioned 1947. Joined Baath Socialist Party. Minister of Interior after Baath *coup d'état* in 1963. Prime Minister, President, Commander-in-chief, Chairman of the Presidency Council 1963–66. Removed by rival *coup d'état* 1966.

HAURANI, Akram (Syria; dates unknown). Sunni Muslim lawyer of Hama. Deputy 1943. Formed Arab Socialist Party 1950. With Michel Aflaq and Salah Bitar formed Baath Socialist Party. President Chamber of Deputies 1957.

HASHIM, Ibrahim Pasha (Jordan; d. 1958). Lawyer, originally from Nablus. Served under Ottoman government before 1914. Moved to Amman after the First World War. Many times Prime Minister of Jordan. Killed in Baghdad in the Iraqi revolution in 1958.

HELOU, Charles (Lebanon; b. 1911). Maronite Christian. Educated at Université St Joseph, and French Law Faculty, Beirut. Lawyer and journalist. Minister in various governments 1949–64. President of the Lebanese Republic 1964.

HUDA, Taufiq abu al (Jordan; d. 1956). Born in Acre, Palestine. Moved to Jordan after the First World War. Chief Secretary to Jordan government 1930. Prime Minister of Jordan for several periods of office.

HUSAIN, HM King (Jordan; b. 1935). Son of HM King Tellal and grandson of King Abdulla of Jordan. Educated in Alexandria, Egypt, and at Harrow School and Royal Military Academy, Sandhurst, England. Became King of Jordan in 1952 at the age of seventeen.

KHURI, Bishara (Lebanon; 1890–1964). Maronite Christian. Leading Lebanese politician during and after the French Mandate. Played an important part in the termination of the Mandate. President of the Republic 1943–52.

226

KHURI, Faris (Syria; 1877–1962). (No relation of Bishara al Khuri). Protestant Christian. Educated Syrian Protestant College (later American University of Beirut). Member of Ottoman Parliament before 1914. Imprisoned by Ottoman government for Arab Nationalist activities. President, Chamber of Deputies 1936–39. Prime Minister 1944–45 and 1954–55.

KUWATLI (Quwatli) Shukri (Syria; b. 1891). Sunni Muslim of Damascus. Nationalist leader during French Mandate. President of the Republic 1943–49. When he was deposed in a military *coup d'état* and sent into exile. President again 1955–58, until incorporation of Syria into the United Arab Republic.

MALIK, Charles (Lebanon; b. 1906). Christian. Educated American University of Beirut and taught there as a Professor. Minister of Foreign Affairs 1956–58. President of the General Assembly of the United Nations 1958–59.

NABULSI, Sulaiman (Jordan; b. 1908). Left-wing Jordan politician. Became Prime Minister in the summer of 1956 after the dismissal of British officers. Favoured a rapprochement with Russia. Lost office April 1957.

QUDSI, Nadhim (Syria; dates unknown). Muslim of Aleppo. Lawyer. Deputy 1943, Prime Minister June 1950. Resigned March 1951. Imprisoned by Shaishakli November 1951. Released February 1952. President of Republic December 1961. Arrested in *coup d'état* March 1962. Resumed presidency May 1962. Arrested after *coup d'état* March 1963. Released from prison December 1963 and retired from politics to Aleppo.

RIFAI, Samir Pasha (Jordan 1901–1966). Born in Palestine, then moved to Trans-Jordan. Prime Minister of Trans-Jordan and of Jordan for several periods.

SHAISHAKLI, Adib (Syria; d. 1964). Sunni Muslim from Hama. Served under French in Syrian Armed Forces. Organized military *coup d'état* at end of 1949, and governed Syria from then until 1954. In 1954 he was deposed by a *coup d'état* and went into exile. In 1964 he was assassinated in Brazil.

SHAMUN (Chamoun) Camille (Lebanon; b. 1900). Maronite Christian of Lebanon. Educated in French Law Faculty Beirut. Member of Lebanese Parliament 1934–52. President of the Lebanese Republic 1952–58. Leader of Liberal National Party.

SHEHAB (Chehab) Fouad (Lebanon; b. 1902). Maronite Christian. Member of the former princely family of the Shihabis. Educated at St Cyr, France. Served under French in the army. Commander-in-chief, Lebanese Armed Forces 1945–58. President of the Republic 1958–64.

SULH, Riyadh (Lebanon; d. 1951). Sunni Muslim from Sidon. A nationalist leader during the French Mandate. Prime Minister 1943–51. Assassinated in July 1951 in Amman, Jordan, by members of the Syrian Populist Party who had followed him from Lebanon.

TELLAL, HM King (Jordan; b. 1908). Son of King Abdulla of Jordan. Became King after his father's assassination on 20 July 1951. Abdicated on 11 August, 1952, owing to ill-health and went to live near Istanbul in Turkey.

TELL, Wasfi (Jordan; b. 1920). Of the Tell family of Irbid in northern Jordan. Prime Minister 1962–63; Minister of Defence 1965.

Index

Numbers in italic refer to illustrations

230

232

233

Rukh, Shah, 101
Russia, Jenghis Khan conquers south, 90; Tamerlane conquers, 99; Russo Turkish War, 108; between the wars, 185